Ferguson
An imprint of Infobase Publishing
132 West 31st Street
New York NY 10001

Library of Congress Cataloging-in-Publication Data

Discovering careers for your future. Construction. — 2nd ed.
    p. cm. — (Discovering careers for your future)
  Includes bibliographical references and index.
  ISBN-13: 978-0-8160-7291-0 (alk. paper)
  ISBN-10: 0-8160-7291-4 (alk. paper)
  1. Building trades—Vocational guidance—Juvenile literature.
  TH159.D57 2008
  690.023--dc22

                                        2007045625

Ferguson books are available at special discounts when purchased in bulk quantities for businesses, associations, institutions, or sales promotions. Please call our Special Sales Department in New York at (212) 967-8800 or (800) 322-8755.

You can find Ferguson on the World Wide Web at http://www.fergpubco.com

Text design by Mary Susan Ryan-Flynn
Cover design by Jooyoung An

Printed in the United States of America

EB MSRF 10 9 8 7 6 5 4 3 2 1

This book is printed on acid-free paper.

Contents

TM

MT

Introduction

You may not have decided yet what you want to be in the future. And you don't have to decide right away. You do know that right now you are interested in building and construction. Do any of the statements below describe you? If so, you may want to begin thinking about what a career in construction might mean for you.

___My favorite class in school is industrial arts/shop.

___I watch television shows on building and renovating homes.

___I like to make or build things.

___I help my parents with household repairs.

___I work with charities that build or renovate homes for those with physical disabilities or financial problems.

___My favorite hobby is woodworking or metalworking.

___I enjoy observing work at construction sites.

___I am good at math.

___I am interested in machines.

___I like to use hand tools and power tools.

___I enjoy helping my parents paint our home.

___I like to design and draw plans for buildings.

___I read how-to books on construction and building.

___I like to figure out how things are made.

___I enjoy studying architecture.

Discovering Careers for Your Future: Construction is a book about careers in construction, from architects to welders. Construction workers design and build homes, schools, office buildings, factories, bridges, roads, and parks. They build basic structures and finish them inside and out, including plastering and painting, installing electricity and plumbing, laying tile, putting in windows, and making cabinets and furniture.

This book describes many possibilities for future careers in construction. Read through it and see how the different careers are connected. For example, if you are interested in designing, you will want to read the chapters on architects and drafters. If you are interested in woodworking, you will want to read the chapters on carpenters and construction laborers. If you are interested in determining costs for major construction projects, you will want to read the chapter on cost estimators. Go ahead and explore!

What Do Construction Workers Do?

The first section of each chapter begins with a heading such as "What Cement Masons Do" or "What Electricians Do." It tells what it's like to work at this job. It describes typical responsibilities and assignments. You will find out about working conditions. Which construction workers work outdoors in all kinds of weather? Which ones work in offices? What kinds of tools and materials do they use? This section answers all these questions.

How Do I Become a Construction Worker?

The section called "Education and Training" tells you what schooling you need for employment in each job—a high school diploma, training at a junior college, a college degree, or more. It also talks about on-the-job training that you could expect to receive after you're hired and whether or not you must complete an apprenticeship program.

How Much Do Construction Workers Earn?

The Earnings section gives the average salary figures for the job described in the chapter. These figures give you a general idea of how much money people with this job can make. Keep in mind that many people really earn more or less than the amounts given here because actual salaries depend on many different things, such as the size of the company, the location of the company, and the amount of education, training, and experience you have. Generally, but not always, bigger companies located in major cities pay more than smaller ones in smaller cities and towns, and people with more education, training, and experience earn more. Also remember that these figures are current averages. They will probably be different by the time you are ready to enter the workforce.

What Will the Future Be Like for Construction Workers?

The Outlook section discusses the employment outlook for the career: whether the total number of people employed in this career will increase or decrease in the coming years and whether jobs in this field will be easy or hard to find. These predictions are based on economic conditions, the size and makeup of the population, foreign competition, and new technology. Phrases such as "faster than the average," "about as fast as the average," and "slower than the average," are used by the U.S. Department of Labor to describe job growth predicted by government data.

Keep in mind that these predictions are general statements. No one knows for sure what the future will be like. Also remember that the employment outlook is a general statement about an industry and does not necessarily apply to everyone. A determined and talented person may be able to find a job in an industry or career with the worst kind of outlook. And a person without ambition and the proper training will find it difficult to find a job in even a booming industry or career field.

Where Can I Find More Information?

Each chapter includes a sidebar called "For More Info." It lists organizations that you can contact to find out more about the field and careers in the field. You will find names, addresses, phone numbers, e-mail addresses, and Web sites.

Extras

Every chapter has a few extras. There are photos that show construction workers in action. There are sidebars and notes on ways to explore the field, fun facts, profiles of people in the field, or lists of additional resources that might be helpful. At the end of the book you will find three additional sections: Glossary, Index of Job Titles, and Browse and Learn More. The Glossary gives brief definitions of words that relate to education, career training, or employment that you may be unfamiliar with. The Index of Job Titles includes all the job titles mentioned in the book. The Browse and Learn More section lists general construction books and Web sites to explore.

It's not too soon to think about your future. We hope you discover several possible career choices. Happy hunting!

Architects

What Architects Do

Architects plan and design buildings and sometimes the land surrounding the buildings. Shopping malls, schools, airports, offices, factories, and homes all began as designs on an

Reach for the Sky

The word "skyscraper" is used to describe any habitable building more than 500 feet tall. Here are the world's 10 tallest buildings, according to the Council on Tall Buildings and Urban Habitat (http://www.ctbuh.org). Height is measured in feet from the sidewalk level of the main entrance to the structural top of the building. Antennae and flag poles are not included.

1. Taipei 101
    Taipei, Taiwan
    1,667 feet, 101 stories

2. Petronas Twin Towers
    Kuala Lumpur, Malaysia
    1,483 feet, 88 stories

3. Sears Tower
    Chicago, United States
    1,451 feet, 110 stories

4. Jin Mao Building
    Shanghai, China
    1,381 feet, 88 stories

5. Two International Finance Centre
    Hong Kong, China
    1,362 feet, 88 stories

6. CITIC Plaza
    Guangzhou, China
    1,283 feet, 80 stories

7. Shun Hing Square
    Shenzhen, China
    1,260 feet, 69 stories

8. Empire State Building
    New York, United States
    1,250 feet, 102 stories

9. Central Plaza
    Hong Kong, China
    1,227 feet, 78 stories

10. Bank of China
    Hong Kong, China
    1,205 feet, 70 stories

Architects review blueprints for an upcoming project.
(Push Pictures, Corbis)

architect's drawing table or computer. Many architects specialize in one kind of building. Some design homes, while others design office buildings, sports arenas, theaters, churches, or manufacturing plants. They may also specialize in interior design or renovations of existing buildings.

Architects begin an assignment by talking with their clients. The clients give the architect information about how much they can afford to spend and the date they would like the building completed. The architect finds out what the client needs and then makes some rough drawings. Eventually, blueprints are prepared that show the exact measurements of every part of the building or area. There will be floor blueprints, wiring blueprints, piping blueprints, and blueprints for the interior and exterior walls. There are usually realistic drawings done of the interior and exterior to show the client what the finished product will look like. For large projects or public buildings, the architect may even construct a small model of the building. Once construction begins, architects visit the site to answer questions and to make sure the builders are following the plans.

Profile: Mies van der Rohe (1886–1969)

Mies van der Rohe was one of the leaders of the International style of architecture. He was known for his elegant but austere steel-and-glass buildings. Classic simplicity and precise proportions mark such works as Crown Hall at the Illinois Institute of Technology (1955); the Dirksen Building, part of the Federal Center in Chicago (1964); and the National Gallery in Berlin (1968).

Mies van der Rohe's buildings at 860 Lake Shore Drive in Chicago, a striking innovation when built in 1951, helped establish the steel skeleton, glass-wall structure as a major building type. His technically efficient, sophisticated style, sometimes called "Miesian," was adapted by architects throughout the Western world.

Architects must be familiar with zoning laws and local and state building regulations, including plumbing, electrical, heating, and ventilation codes. They have to know construction methods and engineering principles. They must also consider the area's climate, soil type, and other environmental conditions. They also use architectural history to see how other architects have solved building design problems in the past.

Education and Training

To prepare for a career as an architect you should take shop classes (especially courses in drafting), math, and art (especially freehand drawing) in high school. History, English, writing, and art history are also important.

To become an architect you must complete a degree program at an architecture school. Most schools of architecture offer degrees through either a five-year bachelor's program, a three- or four-year master's program, or a two-year master of architecture program for students who have earned a preprofessional undergraduate degree in architecture or a related area. The majority of architecture students seek out the bachelor's degree in architecture, going from high school directly into a five-year program.

EXPLORING

○ Books and magazines on architecture will give you a good understanding of the nature of the work.

○ Most architects will welcome the opportunity to talk with you about the field. You may be able to visit their offices to gain a firsthand knowledge of the type of work done by architects.

○ Practice designing and building small structures, such as doll houses, tree houses, and bird houses.

○ You can also build models of larger structures. Your local arts and crafts store may have model building supplies, such as scaled-down furniture, trees and shrubs, flooring, and siding.

○ Take architectural tours in your nearest city and anywhere you vacation.

Earnings

The starting salary for unlicensed interns is $30,000 a year. Newly licensed architects start at around $39,000 a year.

FOR MORE INFO

For more information on careers and schools, contact
American Institute of Architects
1735 New York Avenue NW
Washington, DC 20006-5292
Tel: 800-AIA-3837
E-mail: infocentral@aia.org
http://www.aia.org

For information on careers and membership for high school students, contact
American Institute of Architecture Students
1735 New York Avenue NW
Washington, DC 20006-5292
Tel: 202-626-7472
E-mail: mailbox@aias.org
http://www.aiasorg

For information on careers, schools, and student memberships, contact
Association of Collegiate Schools of Architecture
1735 New York Avenue NW
Washington, DC 20006-5292
Tel: 202-785-2324
E-mail: info@acsa-arch.org
https://www.acsa-arch.org

Architects who are partners in architectural firms or who have their own businesses earn more than $100,000 a year. Partners in some very large firms make more than $130,000.

Outlook

The demand for architects is tied to growth in the office building and home construction industry. Employment for architects will be about the same as the average for other jobs. Competition is stiff in architecture, not only for jobs, but also for acceptance into architectural schools. On the positive side, employment of architects is not likely to be affected by the growing use of computer technologies. Rather than replacing architects, computers are being used to enhance architects' work.

Bricklayers and Stonemasons

What Bricklayers and Stonemasons Do

Bricklayers, sometimes called *brickmasons* and *blockmasons*, construct walls, floors, fireplaces, and other structures with brick, cinder, or concrete block. *Stonemasons* build stone walls and stone exteriors and floors. They usually work on large building projects, such as public buildings, hotels, and office buildings.

Before starting a job, bricklayers and stonemasons work with blueprints (building plans drawn out on paper or by computer) to determine where to construct a wall or other object and how big it should be. To shape bricks and chisel stone, bricklayers and stonemasons use a variety of hand tools, such as hammers, chisels, and brushes. They may also use electric drills and saws.

Bricklayers must know how to mix mortar, which is made of cement, sand, and water, and how to spread it so that the joints throughout the structure will be evenly spaced with a neat appearance. They may have helpers who mix the mortar as well as move materials and scaffolding around the work site.

When laying bricks, bricklayers spread a layer of mortar, place the brick

Did You Know?

○ Sun-baked clay bricks were used in constructing buildings more than 6,000 years ago in Mesopotamia.

○ More than 70 percent of the buildings in the world are made of masonry.

○ Brick is created by firing shale and clay in kilns at approximately 2,000 degrees Fahrenheit.

○ The standard brick size in the United States is 2.5 x 3.75 x 8 inches.

○ Brick homes sell for 6 percent more than homes that are not constructed out of brick.

Source: Mason Contractors Association of America

EXPLORING

○ To become familiar with building materials and to observe the tasks you will perform as a bricklayer or stonemason, visit construction sites or participate in repairs. You can also learn about masonry terms by visiting http://www.masoncontrac tors.org/aboutmasonry/masonry glossary.

○ Ask your shop teacher or guidance counselor to arrange an informational interview with a bricklayer or stonemason.

○ You may also want to join a student organization, such as the National Association of Home Builders Student Chapters Program, where you can learn about the industry as well as take tours and participate in group repairs.

on the mortar bed, and then tap it into place. Care must be taken when starting the building process. Bricklayers continually measure the bricklaying to make sure that it is straight. They cut bricks with a hammer and chisel to fit around windows, doors, and other openings.

When constructing a stone wall or floor, stonemasons set the first level of stones in a layer of mortar. They build a wall by alternating layers of mortar and stone, and they set a stone floor by placing stones over the mortar surface. They use measuring devices so that the work remains straight. To make various shapes and sizes, masons use a special hammer to cut each stone.

Education and Training

In high school, you should take classes in mathematics, mechanical drawing, and blueprint reading, as well as core courses such as English and general science. It is also a good idea to take pre-college engineering classes if your school offers them.

The best way to become a bricklayer or stonemason is to complete a three-year apprenticeship. An apprenticeship will allow you to observe experienced workers and receive classroom instruction. To become an apprentice, you need the approval of the local apprenticeship committee, and you must be at least 17 years old, be in good physical condition, and have a high school diploma.

A mason lays brick in a building that is being restored. (James Marshall, The Image Works)

Earnings

According to the U.S. Department of Labor, the median hourly pay of bricklayers was $20.66 in 2006. A person working full-time at this pay rate would have annual earnings of

To Be a Successful Bricklayer or Stonemason, You Should . . .

○ be detail oriented

○ be able to read blueprints and other building specifications and closely follow instructions

○ be skillful in using hand tools, power tools, and measuring devices

○ not mind getting dirty and working on your hands and knees

○ be able to get along with coworkers as many bricklayers and masons work in teams

FOR MORE INFO

For more information on apprenticeships and training through its National Center for Construction Education and Research, contact
Associated General Contractors of America
2300 Wilson Boulevard, Suite 400
Arlington, VA 22201-5426
Tel: 703-548-3118
E-mail: info@agc.org
http://www.agc.org

For information on apprenticeships and other training opportunities, contact
International Masonry Institute
The James Brice House
42 East Street
Annapolis, MD 21401-1731
Tel: 410-280-1305
http://imiweb.org

For information on masonry and careers in the field, contact
Mason Contractors Association of America
33 South Roselle Road
Schaumburg, IL 60193-1646
Tel: 800-536-2225
http://www.masoncontractors.com

approximately $42,980. Earnings for bricklayers ranged from a low of less than $12.24 per hour (approximately $25,470 annually) to a high of more than $32.43 per hour (about $67,450 yearly) during that same time period.

The U.S. Department of Labor reports the median hourly wage for stonemasons was $17.29 in 2006. This wage translates into annual earnings of approximately $35,960 for full-time work. The lowest paid 10 percent of stonemasons earned less than $10.36 per hour (approximately $21,540 yearly), and the highest paid 10 percent made more than $28.46 hourly (about $59,190 annually).

Of course, earnings for those who work outside can be affected by bad weather, and earnings are lower for workers in areas where the local economy is in a slump. The pay also varies according to geographic region.

The beginning hourly rate for apprentices is about half the rate for experienced workers.

Outlook

Employment for bricklayers and stonemasons is predicted to grow about as fast as the average, according to the U.S. Department of Labor. Job opportunities, however, should be excellent, since many workers leave the field each year for less strenuous work, retirement, or other reasons. In addition, population and business growth will create the need for new facilities (such as homes, hospitals, long-term-care facilities, and offices) and result in a demand for these skilled workers. There will probably be increased construction of many kinds of buildings because of the growing popularity of brick and stone, especially ornamental brickwork and stonework on building fronts and in lobbies.

During economic downturns, bricklayers and stonemasons, like other workers in construction-related jobs, can expect to have fewer job opportunities and perhaps be laid off.

Carpenters

What Carpenters Do

Carpenters cut, shape, and fasten together pieces of wood, wallboard, plywood, and insulation. Most carpenters work on constructing, remodeling, or repairing houses or other buildings. Some carpenters work indoors, some outdoors, and some work both indoors and outdoors. Carpenters work with hand tools, such as hammers, saws, measuring devices, and screwdrivers, and with power tools, such as electric saws and drills.

There are two basic kinds of carpentry work. *Rough carpentry* involves constructing and installing the inner structure of a building, such as the wooden framework of the building and the frames inside walls. The sturdiness of the building depends on how well this is done. Rough carpentry also includes building temporary structures needed on construction sites, such

Tools of the Trade

Cutting and shaping tools. The carpenter's basic cutting tools are *hand-* and *power-operated saws.* The *chisel,* a gouging tool, is important in fitting hardware such as hinges. The *plane* and *sander,* which whittle and smooth wood, are used in interior work and joinery. The *brace-and-bit,* the *hand* or *power drill,* the *gimlet,* and the *awl* are used for boring holes.

Joining tools. The *hammer,* used to drive nails, is the basic joining tool. Wood screws are put in place with a *screwdriver. Clamps* are used to hold two boards together temporarily, especially for gluing.

Measuring tools. The *carpenter's rule* is a folding ruler. The *square* is used for measuring right angles. The *spirit level* indicates when a board is horizontal or vertical. The *plumb line* also indicates vertical position.

as scaffolds, wooden chutes used as channels for wet concrete, and wooden molds or forms that the concrete is poured into to make foundations for buildings.

Finish carpentry involves building and installing wooden floors, shelves, cabinets, and other woodwork. *Finish carpenters* can specialize in one particular structure. *Stair fabricators* and *cabinetmakers* are two types of carpenters with advanced artistic skills in carpentry.

Carpenters remain the largest group of workers in the building trades. There are approximately 1.3 million carpenters in the United States today. The vast majority of them work for contractors involved in building, repairing, and remodeling buildings and other structures. Manufacturing firms, schools, stores, and government bodies employ most other carpenters.

EXPLORING

○ Take classes in woodshop or mechanical drawing.
○ Volunteer for an organization like Habitat for Humanity. Its Youth Programs accept volunteers between the ages of 5 and 25, and its group building projects provide hands-on experience. Contact Habitat for Humanity, 800-422-4828, ext. 2412; youthprograms@habitat.org; http://www.habitat.org/youthprograms.
○ Building sets for a school or community theater can be a fun way to learn simple carpentry skills.
○ Ask your parents to let you help with any home repair or building projects they do.
○ Your local home improvement store may sponsor classes that teach some basic carpentry skills.

Education and Training

A high school education is not required for carpenters, but most contractors and developers prefer you to have a diploma. Classes you should consider taking include carpentry and woodworking, as well as other shop classes; algebra, geometry, and other mathematics courses; science; and mechanical drawing.

After high school, the best way to become a carpenter is to complete a four-year apprenticeship program. Applicants to these programs usually must be high school graduates and at least 17 years old. During training, apprentices work at a

A carpenter (right) *and an apprentice work on a bridge being built over the Grand River in Michigan.* (Jim West, The Image Works)

variety of jobs, learning both rough and finish carpentry. In addition, you receive classroom instruction about different kinds of construction materials; how buildings are built; how to use and care for tools; and how to read blueprints, make sketches, and do the mathematical calculations that are often required on the job.

Many carpenters learn their skills on the job instead of completing an apprenticeship. How thorough your training is depends on your employer and the kinds of experience that the job provides. People who become carpenters in this way sometimes do not learn as much, and it may take them longer to become skilled carpenters, called *journeymen carpenters.*

Earnings

According to the U.S. Department of Labor, the majority of carpenters who did not own their own businesses made between $13.55 and $23.85 an hour in 2006. Wages can range from a low of $10.87 to a high of $30.45 an hour. Starting pay for apprentices is about 40 percent of a journeyman carpenter's wage and increases to 80 percent by the fourth year of training. Apprentices are often hired just for particular projects, rather than as full-time employees.

Outlook

The U.S. Department of Labor predicts that employment for carpenters will grow about as fast as the average. This is because replacement carpenters are needed for the large number of experienced carpenters who leave the field every year for work that is less strenuous. Replacement workers are also needed for the workers just starting out in the field who decide to move on to more comfortable occupations. And, of course, replacements are needed for those who retire. Home modifications for the growing elderly population, two-income couples' desire for larger homes, and the growing population of all ages should contribute to the demand for carpenters.

Tour Norm's Workshop

The PBS and DIY Network television show *The New Yankee Workshop* features master carpenter Norm Abrams. Norm's workshop has a huge variety of tools and equipment, including state-of-the-art inventions. You can take a virtual tour of the workshop at its Web site, http://www.newyankee.com.

Check your local TV listings for other construction how-to shows, such as these:

Curb Appeal
http://www.hgtv.com/hgtv/shows_crb

Hometime
http://www.hometime.com

Handy Ma'am
http://www.pbs.org/wttw/handymaamtv

This Old House
http://www.thisoldhouse.com

Steady employment generally depends on economic conditions in the area where carpenters want to work. In areas where the economy is strong and there is a lot of building going on, well-qualified carpenters can find good job opportunities.

FOR MORE INFO

For more information on apprenticeships and training through its National Center for Construction Education and Research, contact
Associated General Contractors of America
2300 Wilson Boulevard, Suite 400
Arlington, VA 22201-5426
Tel: 703-548-3118
E-mail: info@agc.org
http://www.agc.org

For more information about a career as a carpenter, apprenticeships, contact
Home Builders Institute
1201 15th Street NW, Sixth Floor
Washington, DC 20005-2842
Tel: 800-795-7955
http://www.hbi.org

For information on careers in the construction trades, contact
National Association of Homebuilders
1201 15th Street NW
Washington, DC 20005-2842
Tel: 800-368-5242
http://www.nahb.com

For information on union membership and apprenticeships, contact
United Brotherhood of Carpenters and Joiners of America
Carpenters Training Fund
6801 Placid Street
Las Vegas, NV 89119-4205
http://www.carpenters.org

Cement Masons

What Cement Masons Do

Cement masons are skilled workers who smooth and finish surfaces of concrete on construction projects, ranging from floors and sidewalks to highways, dams, and airport runways. Cement masons are also known as *cement finishers* or *concrete masons.*

At a building site, a cement mason first sets up the forms that will hold the poured concrete until it hardens into the desired shape. After the forms are in place, the mason positions steel rods or mesh in the space where the concrete will be placed. This strengthens the concrete after it dries. Finally, the cement mason pours or directs the pouring of the concrete into the forms. The wet concrete is then spread, leveled, and compacted.

Using a large trowel called a float, cement masons smooth the surface. On driveways, pavements, and similar projects, they finish by brushing the concrete to produce the desired texture. On projects that need curved edges, masons may use tools, such as a curb edger. On walls and floors, they may remove rough or defective spots with a chisel and hammer.

What Is It?

Cement has been used for thousands of years as a hard building material. It is made by mixing such elements as powdered alumina, silica, and limestone with water. Both the ancient Egyptians and the Greeks made cement. The Romans developed a kind of cement made from slaked lime and volcanic ash and used it to build roads, aqueducts, bridges, and other structures.

Joseph Aspdin, an English stonemason, developed the first portland cement mixture in 1824 by burning and grinding together limestone and clay. He called his product "portland" cement because it resembled the limestone quarried on the Isle of Portland. It soon became the most widely used cement because of its strength and resistance to water. Cement manufactured today is essentially made of the same materials as Aspdin's portland cement.

EXPLORING

○ Practice your building skills. Try sculpture, ceramics, or even building sand castles at the beach.

○ Look for construction sites where you might be able to watch cement masons at work.

○ TV shows about home construction and renovation often show how cement masons make foundations, sidewalks, and patios.

○ Talk to a cement mason about his or her career. Ask the following questions: What do you like least and most about your job? How did you train for this field? What advice would you give a young person who is interested in the field?

Smaller projects, such as sidewalks, patios, and driveways, are usually done by hand. On large-scale projects such as highways, power-operated floats and finishing machines are used. Although such large equipment can perform many services, corners and other inaccessible areas usually require hand finishing.

Education and Training

For most jobs in this field, employers try to hire people who are in good physical condition and who have good manual skills. A high school diploma is not required, but it will give you an advantage. Applicants must have completed at least the eighth grade and understand basic math. To qualify as a cement mason, you must also complete either an apprenticeship or an on-the-job training program.

The apprenticeship program consists of two or three years of planned and supervised work experience along with classroom instruction. Apprentices learn the proper way to handle tools, equipment, and materials. They also learn blueprint reading, applied math, estimating procedures, building regulations, and other subjects.

On-the-job training usually requires more time to learn the necessary skills and knowledge than an apprenticeship does. Trainees work under the guidance of experienced masons, often starting as cement helpers or laborers. As you learn job skills, you can move into higher positions.

A World Without Cement?

Today our sidewalks, swimming pools, building foundations, roads, and many other structures are made with cement. Yet there was a period in history—hundreds of years, in fact—when cement was not used at all.

In the Roman Empire during the fifth century, cement was used for building roads, aqueducts, and other structures. After the fall of the Roman Empire, the use of cement in building almost disappeared.

Thirteen centuries passed before John Smeaton, an English engineer, experimented with cement mixtures to develop one that could harden even underwater. He used his cement to build the famous Eddystone Lighthouse, in Devon, England. The Eddystone Rocks are a group of rocks in the English Channel that have caused many shipwrecks. Lighthouses were built at this spot to warn sailors of the danger of hitting the rocks.

The first lighthouse was destroyed by a storm in 1699. The second, made of oak, was destroyed by fire in 1755. Smeaton's tower was built with stone, using cement to bind the stones together. This lighthouse was perhaps the first structure made with cement since the fall of the Roman Empire. The stones and cement began to crumble in the nineteenth century and bronze bolts were used for reinforcement.

Earnings

The U.S. Department of Labor reports that in 2006 most cement masons earned about $25,750 to $43,060 a year. Salaries ranged from less than $20,840 to $56,310 or more. Since the amount of time spent working is limited by weather conditions, many workers' earnings vary from these figures. Cement masons who do not belong to a union generally have lower wages than union workers. Apprentices start at wages that are about 50 to 60 percent of what fully qualified masons earn. They receive periodic raises, so in the last phase of training, their wages are almost as much as an experienced worker's pay.

Outlook

Employment for cement masons is expected to grow about as fast as the average, according to the U.S. Department of

Labor. Construction work is expected to increase during this period, and concrete will be an important building material, especially in nonresidential building and construction.

Work opportunities for masons should be good, since the number of trained workers is relatively small. Cement masons will be in demand to help build roads, bridges, buildings, subways, shopping malls, and many other structures.

FOR MORE INFO

For information on training and apprenticeship programs, contact
Associated General Contractors of America
2300 Wilson Boulevard, Suite 400
Arlington, VA 22201-5426
Tel: 703-548-3118
E-mail: info@agc.org
http://www.agc.org

For information on apprenticeships and other training opportunities, contact
International Masonry Institute
The James Brice House
42 East Street
Annapolis, MD 21401-1731
Tel: 410-280-1305
http://imiweb.org

For information on masonry and careers in the field, contact
Mason Contractors Association of America
33 South Roselle Road
Schaumburg, IL 60193-1646
Tel: 800-536-2225
http://www.masoncontractors.com

For information on masonry, contact
The Masonry Society
3970 Broadway, Suite 201-D
Boulder, CO 80304-1135
E-mail: info@masonrysociety.org
http://www.masonrysociety.org

Construction Inspectors

What Construction Inspectors Do

Construction inspectors make sure that all new structures of any kind—hospitals, schools, housing projects, administrative buildings, bridges, highways, dams, sewer and water systems, military installations, and so on—are built legally, properly, safely, and at a reasonable cost.

Construction inspectors work for local, federal, and state governments as well as for private industries, such as engineering and architectural firms. They visit construction sites, test for defects, and take photographs. They use tape measures, survey instruments, metering devices, and equipment that measures the strength of concrete. They keep records of their work and write reports that tell whether or not the structures are built soundly and meet all the necessary codes and contract specifications. In places where there is danger of

Zoning and Codes

Most buildings must be designed and constructed according to zoning laws and building codes for the communities where they are built.

Zoning laws prevent the construction of certain types of buildings in certain neighborhoods—for example, factories in residential sections. Zoning laws also limit building height and set minimum distances from property lines, so that new buildings do not cut off air and light from adjoining structures.

Building codes are the rules for design and construction that ensure the safety of the occupants. They tell what load a building must be able to withstand and how much fire resistance it must have. Building codes also state the number of exits and stairways required and standards for plumbing, electrical, and mechanical systems.

EXPLORING

○ Offer to help your parents or neighbors with home construction projects. Ask them to teach you how to use hand and power tools.

○ Volunteer to work for theater groups, constructing sets or setting up lights.

○ Field trips to construction sites and interviews with contractors or building trade officials are good ways to learn about what it is like to work in the industry and how best to prepare for it.

○ Take classes offered at your school or community center in woodworking, metalworking, or carpentry.

hurricanes or earthquakes, inspectors check to make sure extra regulations are followed.

There are seven kinds of construction inspectors: building, electrical, elevator, home, mechanical, plumbing, and public works. *Building inspectors* check for structural quality. They look at plans, visit the work site, and make a final inspection when the building is completed. *Electrical inspectors* check all the components of a structure's electrical system, including wiring, lighting, sound and security systems, and generators. *Elevator inspectors* examine not only elevators, but escalators, moving sidewalks in airports, amusement park rides, and ski lifts. *Home inspectors* work for people interested in buying a home. They look at the roof, the pipes, the electrical system, and the plumbing. *Mechanical inspectors* inspect the mechanical parts of gas pipes, gas tanks, and big kitchen appliances. *Plumbing inspectors* check plumbing systems, including how water is supplied to a structure and how waste is removed from it. *Public works inspectors* check all government-built facilities, including water and sewer systems, highways, bridges, dams, and streets to make sure they are safe.

Education and Training

People interested in construction inspection must be high school graduates who have taken courses in drafting, algebra, geometry, and English. Additional shop courses will undoubtedly prove helpful as well.

Government construction inspectors must be high school graduates with a working knowledge of the materials used in construction. Those who have studied engineering or architecture for at least two years in college or those who have attended a community or junior college with courses in construction technology and building inspection will have better chances of finding jobs.

The career of construction inspector is not an entry-level job. Most inspectors receive training on the job and have several years' experience in private industry, either as construction contractors or as carpenters, electricians, plumbers, or pipefitters.

Earnings

Construction and building inspectors earned median salaries of $46,570 a year in 2006, according to the U.S. Department of Labor. Salaries can range from less than $29,210 to $72,590 or more. Salaries in large cities are usually higher than in smaller towns.

Outlook

As the concern for public safety continues to rise, the demand for inspectors should grow faster than the average even if construction activity does not increase. Those who have some college education, are already certified inspectors, or have

What Are Home Inspectors?

Before the 1970s, home inspections were almost unheard of in residential real estate transactions. Buyers made decisions based on their own impressions of the home and the reports of the seller's real estate agent. A residential real estate boom in the late 1990s created a huge demand for home inspectors.

Today, home buyers have the right to order one or more professional inspections of the home before they complete the purchase. Home inspectors must report on the condition of a home's major systems, components, and structure, including the presence of hazardous materials, such as asbestos and lead-based paint.

experience as carpenters, electricians, or plumbers will have the best opportunities. Construction and building inspectors tend to be older, more experienced workers who have worked in other construction occupations for many years.

FOR MORE INFO

For additional information on a career as a construction inspector, contact the following organizations.

American Construction Inspectors Association
12995 6th Street, Suite 69
Yucaipa, CA 92399-2549
Tel: 888-867-2242
E-mail: office@acia.com
http://www.acia.com

American Society of Home Inspectors
932 Lee Street, Suite 101
Des Plaines, IL 60016-6546
Tel: 800-743-2744
http://www.ashi.com

International Code Council
500 New Jersey Avenue NW, 6th Floor
Washington, DC 20001-2070
Tel: 888-422-7233
http://www.iccsafe.org

Construction Laborers

What Construction Laborers Do

Construction laborers are part of a team that builds homes, offices, highways, bridges, apartment buildings, and other structures. They load and unload bricks and other materials, clean up rubble, and pour and spread concrete. They bring tools, materials, and equipment to other workers at a construction site. They may set up scaffolding, dig trenches, and build braces to support the sides of excavations. They work with carpenters, electricians, plumbers, bricklayers, and stonemasons, carrying their equipment and assisting in other ways. Sometimes they operate heavy machinery, such as jackhammers, cement mixers, front-end loaders, hoists, and laser beam equipment used to align and grade ditches and tunnels.

The tasks of construction laborers are physically demanding and repetitive. Not only do they have to lift and carry heavy objects, they also have to crouch and crawl into awkward positions. Sometimes they have to work high up off the ground, and, because they most often work outdoors, they must be prepared to work in all kinds of weather.

Laborers are trained in the methods, materials, and operations used in all kinds of construction work. They must always follow safety procedures. They are sometimes exposed to harmful chemicals, fumes, and odors, or to dangerous machinery, and they must wear special safety clothing and helmets.

Education and Training

Although no formal education is needed to become a laborer, only those with at least a high school education are likely to

EXPLORING

○ Learn how to use hand tools and power tools.
○ Working on any construction or carpentry project can give you experience.
○ Offer to help your parents and neighbors with projects, such as building a deck or patio, building a home addition, putting in a new sidewalk, or remodeling a kitchen.

have a chance to become supervisors or advanced workers (such as carpenters, bricklayers, and stonemasons).

The best way to become a construction laborer is to apply directly to local contractors. You must be at least 18 years old, in good physical condition, and show a willingness and ability to learn. Laborers then receive on-the-job training.

Apprenticeships give you the opportunity to acquire specialized skills. They usually last two to three years and are sponsored by local unions and contractors.

Earnings

According to the U.S. Department of Labor, the median hourly wage for construction laborers was $12.66 in 2006. The lowest paid laborers made less than $8.16 an hour, and the highest paid earned $24.19 an hour or more. It is rare that a laborer finds full-time, year-round work, since construction is seasonal in most parts of the country.

What Is Prefab?

In a simple type of prefabrication, the joists, studs, and window and door frames of a wooden frame house are cut in a factory and delivered to the building site for assembly. Precast concrete refers to prefabricated concrete beams, floor slabs, walls, and other structures. With some prefabrication methods, large sections of a building or even entire houses are built in a factory. In modular construction, large box-like sections of a building are built to standard sizes. Each section may contain several rooms complete with all windows, doors, fixtures, and other parts. The sections are shipped to the building site, where they are joined.

Prefabrication offers the possibility of lower costs through the use of mass production methods, but it is often offset by high shipping and handling costs.

Laborers who belong to the Laborers' International Union of North America tend to receive better pay and benefits than nonunion workers.

Outlook

Construction is a large industry, and turnover is high among laborers. For these reasons, every year there will be jobs available, mainly in connection with large projects. In addition, construction activity is always affected by economic conditions. Regions that are prosperous will offer better job possibilities for construction laborers than areas where the economy is not expanding.

The U.S. Department of Labor predicts that employment for construction laborers will grow more slowly than the average. Opportunities will be best for laborers with experience and specialized training in lead, asbestos, and other hazardous materials removal.

FOR MORE INFO

The Associated General Contractors of America is a trade association that can give you more information about the building industry and life at a construction site.

Associated General Contractors of America
2300 Wilson Boulevard, Suite 400
Arlington, VA 22201-5426
Tel: 703-548-3118
E-mail: info@agc.org
http://www.agc.org

The Laborers' International Union can provide you with materials describing union benefits.

Laborers' International Union of North America
905 16th Street NW
Washington, DC 20006-1703
Tel: 202-737-8320
http://www.liuna.org

Cost Estimators

What Cost Estimators Do

Cost estimators figure out how much it will cost to build or make something. Builders and manufacturers need cost estimators when they plan a new project or a new product. Since they may deal with budgets in the millions of dollars, cost estimators must have good judgment.

First, a builder shows the plans to a cost estimator. The cost estimator looks them over and carefully thinks about all the things that will go into the large building project. Some questions that the cost estimator must think about include: How much will the builder have to pay for labor? What equipment will the builder have to buy or rent? What materials will be needed, and how much will they cost? How much will it cost to bring all the materials to the building site?

Cost estimators must gather the necessary information to answer all these questions. Then, they put together an estimate. If a project is very complicated, there may be a need for several cost estimators to handle different parts of the project. For example, one estimator may work only on the cost of electrical work, while another covers the cost of transportation. The *chief estimator* puts all these separate reports together and forms one complete estimate.

Estimators working for manufacturers have to figure out how much it will cost to train workers to produce a new product. They must determine what parts and materials cost. They must also estimate how much labor will be needed to make the product. Because a manufacturer will probably be making the product for years, estimators must also predict how fast these costs will rise. They must consider what equipment is needed and how quickly the equipment will wear out and have to be replaced.

If a builder or manufacturer needs an estimate in a hurry, the cost estimator has to work long hours to get it done on time. Because estimators may have to make decisions very quickly, they must work well under pressure.

Education and Training

If you are interested in a career as a cost estimator, take courses in mathematics, English, and speech in high school. Shop and drafting classes will also be helpful. It is essential that you are good at math, since a large part of your job will involve comparing calculations.

Builders and manufacturers want cost estimators to know all about their particular business. For this reason, on-the-job training is important for any cost estimator. Many cost estimators begin as tradespeople, such as carpenters or plumbers. Here they gain experience in figuring out how much a given job will cost, and then they switch to a cost estimator position.

Many technical schools and community colleges offer two-year programs that specialize in manufacturing and construction processes. Accounting and business courses are also helpful. The federal government and some other employers require you to have a bachelor's degree in either civil engineering or mathematics.

EXPLORING

○ Learn terms used in the field. The Society of Cost Estimating and Analysis offers a glossary of terms at its Web site, http://www.sceaonline.org/prof_dev/glossary.cfm.

○ One way to prepare for a career as a cost estimator is to create budgets for events, either at home or at school. Then, evaluate the accuracy of the budget after the event or project is completed.

○ Watching the construction of a building or taking a factory tour will give you an idea of all the different kinds of workers, materials, and equipment involved.

○ Another way to discover more about career opportunities is simply by talking to a professional cost estimator. Ask your school counselor to help arrange an interview with an estimator to ask questions about his or her job demands, work environment, and personal opinion of the job.

To Be a Successful Cost Estimator, You Should . . .

○ have strong mathematical and analytical skills

○ work well with others

○ be confident and assertive when presenting findings to engineers, business owners, and design professionals

○ have excellent communication skills

Earnings

Salaries vary according to the size of the construction or manufacturing firm and the experience and education of the worker. According to the U.S. Department of Labor, the median annual salary for cost estimators was $52,940 in 2006. The lowest 10 percent earned less than $31,600 and the highest 10 percent earned more than $88,310. Starting salaries for graduates of engineering or construction management programs were

Mean Annual Earnings for Cost Estimators by Industry, 2006

Computer and peripheral equipment manufacturing:	$73,820
Wired telecommunications carriers:	$70,840
Scientific research and development services:	$69,260
Nonresidential building construction:	$64,550
Building equipment contractors:	$59,470
Residential building construction:	$56,280
Foundation, structure, and building exterior contractors:	$56,170
Building finishing contractors:	$55,640

Source: U.S. Department of Labor

higher than those with degrees in other fields. A salary survey by the National Association of Colleges and Employers reports that candidates with degrees in construction science/management were offered average starting salaries of $42,923 a year in 2005.

Outlook

Employment for cost estimators is expected to increase faster than the average, according to the U.S. Department of Labor. As in most industries, highly trained college graduates and those with the most experience have the best job prospects.

Many jobs will arise from the need to replace workers leaving the industry, either to retire or change jobs. The construction industry will provide the largest number of job openings. The fastest growing areas in construction are in special trade and government projects, including the building and repairing of highways, streets, bridges, subway systems, airports, waterways, and electrical plants.

In manufacturing, employment is predicted to remain stable. Estimators will be in demand because employers will continue to need their services to control operating costs.

Because the work of cost estimators depends entirely on manufacturing and construction, the employment of cost estimators is sensitive to economic fluctuations. This will continue to be true over the next 10 years.

FOR MORE INFO

For information on a career as a cost estimator, contact the following organizations.

AACE International
209 Prairie Avenue, Suite 100
Morgantown, WV 26501-5934
Tel: 800-858-2678
E-mail: info@aacei.org
http://www.aacei.org

American Society of Professional Estimators
2525 Perimeter Place Drive, Suite 103
Nashville, TN 37214-3674
Tel: 615-316-9200
E-mail: info@aspenational.com
http://www.aspenational.com

Society of Cost Estimating and Analysis
527 Maple Avenue East, Suite 301
Vienna, VA 22180-4753
Tel: 703-938-5090
E-mail: scea@sceaonline.net
http://www.sceaonline.net

Drafters

What Drafters Do

Drafters are technical artists who prepare clear, complete, and accurate drawings for engineering and manufacturing purposes. These drawings are based on the rough sketches and calculations of engineers, architects, and industrial designers. To complete their drawings, drafters use their knowledge of machinery, engineering practices, mathematics, building materials, and the physical sciences.

For example, an architect might prepare a rough sketch of an office building. The sketch shows what the building will look like and includes its dimensions—the measurements of its size. However, before the building can be constructed, extremely detailed drawings of every part of the building must be made. These drawings, called *blueprints* or *layouts,* are created by drafters.

Mechanical Drawing Technique

The most common type of mechanical drawing uses orthographic projection. A projection is a view. In the orthographic projection the top, front, and end views of an object are presented in true shape and exact scale. An object drawn in perspective looks distorted. Since an orthographic projection is drawn to scale, its dimensions can be easily checked with a ruler. This cannot be done with a perspective view because distant objects appear to be closer together than they really are.

There are two general types of orthographic projection. An *assembly drawing* shows the entire object, with small drawings illustrating how the various parts are put together. The *detail drawing* shows each individual part of the object separately.

Drafters have different levels of responsibility. *Senior drafters,* sometimes called *chief drafters,* use the ideas of architects and engineers to make design layouts. *Detailers* make complete drawings from these design layouts. Complete drawings usually include the dimensions of the object shown and the type of material to be used in constructing it. *Checkers* carefully examine drawings to look for mistakes.

Drafters often specialize in a certain type of drawing or in a certain field. *Commercial drafters* do all-around drafting, such as plans for building sites or layouts of offices or factories. *Cartographic drafters* help with accurate mapmaking, focusing on political boundaries and borders. *Geological drafters* make diagrams and maps of geological formations and locations of mineral, oil, and gas deposits. *Architectural drafters* create drawings of buildings and other structures. They may specialize by type of structure (residential, commercial, school, etc.) or the material used (reinforced concrete, steel, etc.). *Civil drafters* focus on creating drawings for major construction or civil engineering projects. *Electrical drafters* make schematics and wiring diagrams to be used by construction crews working on equipment and wiring in power plants, communications centers, buildings, or electrical distribution systems. *Electronics drafters* draw schematics and wiring diagrams for television cameras and TV sets, radio transmitters and receivers, computers, radiation detectors, and other electronic equipment.

EXPLORING

○ Participate in hobbies that require the use of drawings or blueprints, such as woodworking, building models, and remodeling projects.

○ Experiment with computer-aided design and drafting programs.

○ When your family purchases an item that you put together yourself, take a close look at the assembly instructions and drawings. Examine other drawn instructions, such as those that explain how to operate a DVD player.

○ Practice your drawing skills. Try to explain a simple task using only pictures, no words. For example, draw a series of pictures that instruct someone how to make a peanut butter and jelly sandwich. Then ask a friend or family member to follow your visual instructions. Did you get a peanut butter and jelly sandwich, or did you invent a new recipe?

Mechanical drafters make working drawings of machinery, automobiles, power plants, or any mechanical device.

For many years, drafters traditionally worked at large, tilted drawing tables, with a variety of drawing instruments, including protractors, compasses, triangles, squares, drawing pens, and pencils. Today, most drafters use computer-aided design and drafting (known as CADD) systems.

Education and Training

A drafter needs a solid background in mathematics and science. Mechanical drawing classes and wood, metal, or electric shop are also very important. English classes will improve your communication skills.

Profile: Gaspard Monge (1746–1818)

Gaspard Monge's concepts of descriptive geometry helped develop drafting as a profession. His interest in describing the world around him inspired him to develop new instruments for surveying topography. He used these tools to make a large-scale plan of his hometown of Beaune, France. The plan drew the attention of the École de Militaire de Mézières, a military academy, where he was accepted as a draftsman. He astounded his teachers when he substituted geometric methods for the standard arithmetical approach to computing the proper locations for gun placements for a proposed fortress. His new method obtained the result so quickly that his commander at first refused it. After consideration, it became a highly guarded military secret for more than 30 years.

Monge's *Géométrie Descriptive* was developed from lectures he gave at engineering schools in the years around the turn of the nineteenth century. It expanded on his method for representing a solid in three-dimensional space on a two-dimensional plane by drawing its projections, known as planes, elevations, and traces. Another text, *Feuilles d'analyse appliqué à la géométrie (Analysis Applied to Geometry)*, established the geometric methods of algebraic geometry. Monge's theories revolutionized engineering design and changed mathematics education significantly.

Most beginning drafters must have some training after high school to get a job. You can enroll in drafting programs offered by community colleges. These two-year programs include courses in science, mathematics, drawing, sketching, and drafting techniques. Most employers today prefer to hire graduates of four-year programs at technical institutes.

Earnings

The U.S. Department of Labor reports the following median salaries for drafters by specialty in 2006: architectural and civil drafters, $41,960; electrical and electronics drafters, $46,830; and mechanical drafters, $43,700. Salaries for all drafters ranged from less than $26,000 to $74,000 or more annually.

FOR MORE INFO

For career information, contact
American Design Drafting Association
105 East Main Street
Newbern, TN 38059-1526
Tel: 731-627-0802
http://www.adda.org

The IFPTE is the union associated with the drafting community.
International Federation of Professional and Technical Engineers (IFPTE)
8630 Fenton Street, Suite 400
Silver Spring, MD 20910-3828
Tel: 301-565-9016
http://www.ifpte.org

Outlook

The U.S. Department of Labor predicts that employment for drafters will increase more slowly than the average. Increasing use of CADD technology will limit the demand for less skilled drafters, but industrial growth and more complex designs of new products and manufacturing processes will increase the demand for drafting services. It is important to remember that during times of slow economic growth, fewer buildings and manufactured products are designed, and therefore, fewer drafters may be needed.

Drywall Installers and Finishers

What Drywall Installers and Finishers Do

Drywall panels consist of a thin layer of plaster between two sheets of heavy paper. The panels are used in place of wet plaster to make the inside walls and ceilings of houses and other buildings. *Drywall installers* measure the areas to be covered, mark the panels, and cut them. They use a keyhole saw to cut openings for electrical outlets, vents, and plumbing fixtures. Next, they fit the pieces of drywall into place and use glue to attach them to the wooden framework. Finally, they nail or screw them down. Installers usually need a helper to move the larger, heavier, more awkward pieces of drywall.

Large ceiling panels may have to be raised with a special lift. After the drywall is in place, installers usually attach metal frames, also called beading, on the edges of the walls. They also attach the trim for windows, doorways, and vents.

Drywall finishers, also called *tapers,* seal and hide the joints where drywall panels come together and prepare the walls for painting or wallpapering. They mix a quick-drying sealing compound and spread the paste into and over the joints with a special trowel or spatula. While the paste is still wet, the finishers press paper tape over the joint and press

Plaster Facts

- Drywall is the main material used in the United States for interior walls.
- Drywall is also called gypsum board, wallboard, plasterboard, gypboard, and rock.
- Gypsum is calcium sulfate dihydrate ($CaSO_4$ $2H_2O$), a naturally occurring mineral that is mined in dried ancient seabeds.

it down. When the sealer is dry, they spread a cementing material over the tape. They blend this material into the wall to hide the joint. Sometimes finishers have to apply second or third coats of sealer to smooth out all the rough areas on the walls. Any cracks or holes and nail and screw heads in the walls or ceiling are filled with sealer.

With a final sanding of the patched areas, the walls and ceiling are ready to be painted or papered. Some finishers apply textured surfaces to walls and ceilings. To do so, they use trowels, brushes, rollers, or spray guns.

Education and Training

Most employers prefer to hire applicants with a high school diploma. Drywall installers and finishers are trained on the job. Installers begin as helpers to experienced workers. At first, they carry materials, hold panels, and clean up. After a few weeks, they learn to measure, cut, and install panels. Finisher helpers start out by taping joints and sealing nail holes and scratches. Then they learn to install corner guards and to hide openings around pipes. Both installers and finishers also learn to estimate job costs.

Another way to learn this trade is through apprenticeship programs. Such programs combine classroom study with on-the-job training.

Earnings

According to the U.S. Department of Labor, the median hourly wage of drywall installers and finishers was $17.38 in 2006, which would amount to about $36,140 a year for full-time employment. Annual salaries range from less than $22,680 to

EXPLORING

○ Learn more about drywall installers and finishers by reading books and magazines and surfing the Internet.
○ It may be possible to visit a job site and observe installers and finishers at work. Ask your shop teacher to help arrange such a visit.
○ Once you get to high school, summer employment as a helper to drywall workers, carpenters, or painters or even as a laborer on a construction job will help you to get some practical experience in this field.

A drywall installer uses a pole sander to smooth the surface of drywall. (David Lassman, Syracuse Newspapers, The Image Works)

$60,010 or more a year. Those workers who have managerial duties or own their own businesses may make even more. Apprentices generally receive about half the rate earned by journeymen workers.

Some drywallers are paid by the hour. Others are paid based on how much work they complete. For example, a contractor might pay installers and finishers five to six cents for every square foot of panel installed. The average worker is capable of installing 35 to 40 panels a day, when each panel measures 4 feet by 12 feet ($83.50 to $110.40 per day).

Outlook

The U.S. Department of Labor predicts job growth for drywall installers and finishers to be slower than the average. This slow

A Bit of History

When the Great Pyramid of Cheops was built nearly 4,500 years ago, the Egyptians used gypsum plaster to decorate the surfaces of its interior passages and rooms. But gypsum plaster is difficult to work with because it may harden before it can be properly applied.

The Greeks used selenite gypsum for windows for their temples because of its transparent quality. The writer Theophrastus (372–287 B.C.) described quite precisely the fabrication of plaster as it was done at that time in Syria and Phoenicia.

The Romans used plaster to cast many thousands of copies of Greek statues.

In the 1700s, Paris became the "capital of plaster," since all the walls of wooden houses were covered with plaster to protect against fire. The king of France had enforced this rule after the Great Fire of London in 1666. Large gypsum deposits near Paris have long been mined to manufacture "plaster of paris."

It wasn't until around 1900 that additives began to be used to control the setting time of gypsum, which led to modern plastering techniques and products.

Mean Annual Earnings for Drywall Installers and Finishers by Industry, 2006

Foundation, structure, and building exterior contractors:	$41,010
Nonresidential building construction:	$39,090
Building finishing contractors:	$38,820
Residential building construction:	$37,740

Source: U.S. Department of Labor

growth rate, however, does not mean qualified workers will be unable to find work. Drywall is much cheaper and faster to install than plaster. High turnover in this field, due to workers leaving for different jobs, means new workers are needed every year. Jobs will be more plentiful in and around cities, where contractors have enough business to hire full-time drywall workers. In small towns, carpenters often do drywall installation and painters do the finishing.

FOR MORE INFO

This trade association has information on the construction industry and educational opportunities.
Associated Builders and Contractors
4250 North Fairfax Drive, 9th Floor
Arlington, VA 22203-1607
Tel: 703-812-2000
E-mail: gotquestions@abc.org
http://www.abc.org

For career and training information for painters, drywall finishers, and others, contact
International Union of Painters and Allied Trades
1750 New York Avenue NW
Washington, DC 20006-5301
Tel: 202-637-0700
E-mail: mail@iupat.org
http://www.iupat.org

Electricians

What Electricians Do

Electricians install and repair the wiring and electrical equipment that supplies light, heat, refrigeration, air-conditioning, and other electrical services, as well as telecommunications equipment. Electricians work on new construction and remodeling projects. They make electrical repairs in homes, offices, factories, and other businesses. They install many types of switches, controls, circuit breakers, wires, lights, signal devices, and electrical parts. Electricians usually specialize in either construction or maintenance.

Most *construction electricians* are employed by contractors or builders. Others have their own companies. Some work for large industrial plants or state highway departments.

Words to Learn

capacitance the ability to store charge; measured in farads (F)

charge a unit of energy; measured in coulombs

current a measure of electric flow; measured in amperes

energy measured in joules or electron volts (eV)

frequency measured in cycles per second or hertz (Hz)

inductance the ability of a conductor to induce voltage when the current changes, measured in henrys (H)

power the rate of energy flowing; measured in watts or (J/SecHp)

resistance measure of opposition to flow of electricity, kind of like friction for the electrons; measured in ohms

To install wiring, construction electricians bend conduit (metal pipe or tubing that holds wiring) so that it will attach snugly to walls, floors, or beams. Then they pull insulated wires or cables through the conduit and connect the wires or cables to circuit breakers, fuse boxes, transformers, or other components. Finally, they test the circuit to be sure that it is grounded, that the connections are properly made, and that the circuits are not overloaded.

Maintenance electricians do periodic inspections to find and fix problems. They check the reliability of electrical equipment, such as motors, electronic controls, and telephone wiring. They make necessary repairs and change defective fuses, switches, circuit breakers, and wiring.

Many maintenance electricians work for manufacturing industries such as those that produce automobiles, ships, steel, chemicals, or machinery. Others work for city governments, shopping centers, or housing complexes. Some maintenance electricians have their own shops.

EXPLORING

- ○ Hobbies such as repairing radios, building electronics kits, or working with model electric trains will build skills that you will use as an electrician.
- ○ Join school science clubs. Work on science-fair projects that focus on electricity and electronics.
- ○ Talk to an electrician about his or her career. Ask the following questions: What do you like least and most about your job? How did you train for this field? What advice would you give a young person who is interested in the field?
- ○ Check your library or bookstore for materials on electricity.

Education and Training

A high school education is the first step toward a career in this field. Most electricians agree that the best way to learn the trade is through an apprenticeship program. To get into an apprenticeship program, you must be between 17 and 24 years old, and you must take tests to determine your aptitude for the trade. Most apprenticeship programs involve four years of

An electrician installs a fire alarm in a building that is under construction. (Jeff Greenberg, The Image Works)

on-the-job training in which you work for several electrical contractors in different types of work. Apprentices learn to operate, care for, and safely handle the tools, equipment, and materials commonly used in the trade.

Earnings

Most electricians working for contractors earn between $21 and $22 an hour, or between $43,680 and $45,760 per year. Beginning apprentices earn 40 to 50 percent of the base electrician's wage and receive increases each year of their apprenticeship. Those who work as telecommunications or residential specialists tend to make slightly less than those who work as linemen or wiremen.

According to the U.S. Department of Labor, the highest paid electricians earned more than $34.95 an hour in 2006. The lowest paid electricians earned less than $12.76 an hour.

Women in Electrical Construction

In the last several years, women have taken an increasing number of jobs in construction—as contractors, foremen, project managers, and supervisors, but also as electricians and apprentices. As of December 31, 2006, more than 1.1 million women were employed in the U.S. construction industry—an increase of nearly 5 percent from 2005. Several organizations offer assistance to women who aspire to work in or who are currently employed in the construction industry, including the National Association of Women in Construction (http://www.nawic.org) and Women In Non-Traditional Employment Roles (http://www.winterwomen.org).

Outlook

The U.S. Department of Labor predicts that employment of electricians will grow about as fast as the average. Growth will be driven by the ever-expanding use of electrical and electronic devices and equipment. Electricians will be called on to upgrade old wiring and to install and maintain more extensive wiring systems than have been necessary in the past. In particular, the use of sophisticated computer, telecommunications, and data-processing equipment and automated manufacturing systems is expected to lead to job opportunities for electricians.

Construction activity fluctuates depending on the state of the local and national economy. Thus, during economic slow-downs, opportunities for construction electricians may not be plentiful. People working in this field need to be prepared for periods of unemployment between construction projects.

Did You Know?

○ Approximately 656,000 electricians are employed in the United States.
○ Ten percent of electricians are self-employed.

Source: U.S. Department of Energy

FOR MORE INFO

For information on union membership, contact
International Brotherhood of Electrical Workers
900 Seventh Street NW
Washington, DC 20001-3886
Tel: 202-833-7000
http://www.ibew.org

For information on certification, contact
International Society of Certified Electronic Technicians
3608 Pershing Avenue
Fort Worth, TX 76107-4527
Tel: 800-946-0201

E-mail: info@iscet.org
http://www.iscet.org

For industry information, contact
National Electrical Contractors Association
3 Bethesda Metro Center, Suite 1100
Bethesda, MD 20814-6302
Tel: 301-657-3110
http://www.necanet.org

For additional information on training to become an electrician, contact
National Joint Apprenticeship and Training Committee
http://www.njatc.org

Glaziers

What Glaziers Do

Glaziers install window glass, mirrors, structural glass, store fronts, walls, doors, and ceilings. They also install skylights, tables, showcases, automobile windows, shower doors, and tub enclosures. In most cases, glass is precut to size in a shop or factory and comes to the work site mounted in a frame. Because glass is heavy and easily breakable, glaziers may need to use a hoist or a crane to move larger pieces into position. The glass is held with suction cups and gently guided into place.

When it is in place, glaziers often put the glass on a bed of putty or another kind of cement inside a metal or wooden

How Glass Is Formed

Glassmaking takes two main steps: (1) heating and mixing raw materials to produce molten glass, and (2) forming the molten glass into the desired shape. Most glass then receives further treatment to produce the final product.

In a process called *drawing,* which produces flat-drawn glass, a horizontal wire called a *bait* is lowered into molten glass and then raised. Glass sticks to the wire and is drawn upward as a continuous sheet. Once hardened, the glass is cut into sheets for use in windows and inexpensive mirrors.

In a process called *floating,* molten glass is allowed to flow onto a bath of molten tin and then allowed to cool. The tin has a low melting point and remains liquid at temperatures at which the glass hardens. The surface of the metal leaves the glass with a very smooth surface. Float glass is used in windows and other flat glass products.

Other forming processes include *blowing* (to make bottles), *pressing* (to make drinking glasses and heat-resistant glassware), and *rolling* (to produce flat glass that does not require a fine finish, such as glass made with a figured pattern on its surface).

frame. They secure the glass with metal clips, metal or wooden molding, bolts, or other devices. They may put a rubber gasket around the outside edges to clamp the glass in place and make a moisture-proof seal. Glaziers sometimes pack a putty-like glazing compound into the joints at the edges of the glass in the molding that surrounds the open space. They trim off the excess compound with a glazing knife for a neat appearance.

Sometimes glaziers manually cut glass by hand to size at a work site. They put uncut glass on a rack or cutting table and measure and mark the cutting line. They use a cutting tool such as a small, sharp wheel of hard metal, which cuts the glass when rolled firmly over the surface. After making a cut, they break off the excess by hand or with a notched tool.

EXPLORING

○ Take up a hobby, such as stained glass, making windowpanes, lampshades, and ornaments. Glass etching can teach you about the properties of glass and how to handle it. Making mosaics using either glass or ceramic tiles gives you practice in cutting and adhering tiles to other surfaces.

○ For a more direct look at this career, you may be able to get a part-time or summer job as a helper at a construction site or in a glass shop. If this cannot be arranged, it may be possible to talk with someone employed in a glass shop or as a glazier in construction work to get an insider's view of the field.

Glaziers may work for construction companies, glass suppliers, or glazing contractors. Some work in factories where they assemble windows or other glass products. They may work outside at a building site or indoors. Often they work on platforms at great heights, and sometimes they may drive a truck that carries the glass and tools to the job.

Education and Training

Most employers prefer to hire high school graduates as glaziers. Glaziers must complete either an apprenticeship or an on-the-job training program. The apprenticeship program lasts between three and four years. It includes shop training as well

Facts About the Construction Industry

○ The construction industry is one of the largest industries in the United States.

○ More than 7 million people are employed in the field.

○ There are approximately 818,000 construction establishments in the United States. Sixty-three percent of these businesses were specialty trade contractors; 30 percent were building construction contractors; and 7 percent were heavy and civil engineering construction or highway contractors.

○ Employment in the field is expected to grow by 11 percent from 2004 to 2014.

Source: U.S. Department of Labor

as classroom study. Glaziers who learn their skills on the job usually begin as helpers to experienced workers and gradually learn to do more difficult tasks. Their training lasts four or more years. Most glaziers belong to a union.

Earnings

According to the U.S. Department of Labor, glaziers earned median salaries of $34,610 in 2006. Wages ranged from less than $21,190 to $63,490 or more. Glaziers who work under union contracts usually make more money than workers who are not union members. A recent study showed that earnings also vary

Is Glass a Solid?

Glass is formed when certain substances are cooled rapidly and do not crystallize. That means their atoms do not arrange themselves in a repeating, orderly pattern. Instead, the atoms become fixed in a disorganized pattern characteristic of the atoms of a liquid. In fact, scientists refer to glass as a liquid. The liquid in glass, however, is of a very high viscosity (resistance to flowing), so glass is a rigid material.

depending on your location. For example, union glaziers in Birmingham, Alabama, earn lower wages than those in New York City. Bad weather, periods of unemployment, and other factors can affect the number of hours glaziers work. Wages for apprentices usually start at about 40 to 50 percent of the skilled glazier's rate and increase periodically throughout the training period.

Outlook

The U.S. Department of Labor predicts that employment for glaziers will increase about as fast as the average. This is due to growth in residential and nonresidential construction and the demand for specialized safety glass and glass coated with protective laminates. Glass will most likely continue to be a popular construction material for both its good looks and its practical advantages.

FOR MORE INFO

For career and training information for glaziers and others, contact
International Union of Painters and Allied Trades
1750 New York Avenue NW
Washington, DC 20006-5301
Tel: 202-637-0700
E-mail: mail@iupat.org
http://www.iupat.org

For information on glassmaking, contact
National Glass Association
8200 Greensboro Drive, Suite 302
McLean, VA 22102-3881
Tel: 866-342-5642
http://www.glass.org

Heating and Cooling Technicians

What Heating and Cooling Technicians Do

Heating and cooling technicians install, repair, and service the machinery that heats and cools buildings. Since each heating and cooling system involves more than one machine, technicians must understand every part, including the ducts and pipes that distribute the air throughout a building. Some technicians are trained in all aspects of the field, but many specialize in a certain area. Technicians work in factories, supermarkets, hotels, and stores, and at new construction sites.

Technicians who assemble and install air-conditioning, refrigeration, and heating systems and equipment work from blueprints. Because structure sizes and climate-control specifications vary, technicians have to pay close attention to blueprint details. They use algebra and geometry to calculate the sizes and shapes of duct work.

As a final step in assembly and installation, technicians run tests on equipment to ensure that it functions properly. They adjust thermostats, reseal piping, and replace parts as needed.

Some heating and cooling technicians work for companies that manufacture air-conditioning, heating, and refrigeration equipment. Here they may

Did You Know?

○ Approximately 270,000 heating and cooling technicians are employed in the United States.

○ Florida, New Jersey, Maryland, and Massachusetts employ the most heating and cooling technicians.

○ Approximately 16 percent of heating and cooling technicians are members of a union.

○ Fifteen percent of all heating and cooling technicians are self-employed.

Source: U.S. Department of Labor

test or help design new equipment. Other technicians work for companies that sell, install, and repair the equipment. These technicians help customers select equipment that best suits their needs.

In their work on refrigerant lines and air ducts, heating and cooling technicians use a variety of hand and power tools, including hammers, wrenches, metal snips, electric drills, pipe cutters and benders, and acetylene torches. To check electrical circuits, burners, and other components, technicians work with volt-ohmmeters, manometers, and other testing devices.

EXPLORING

○ Check out http://www.coolcareers.org, a Web site created by a coalition of organizations representing the heating, air-conditioning, and refrigeration industry.

○ If you are interested in a career as a heating and cooling technician, ask your shop teacher to arrange field trips to companies that manufacture or repair this equipment.

○ Visiting a technical school that offers air-conditioning, refrigeration, and heating classes also can be very helpful.

Education and Training

To become a heating and cooling technician, you must earn a high school diploma. Some high school courses that will help prepare you for this career are English, computer science, physics, algebra, and geometry. Courses in mechanical drawing, blueprint reading, and metal shop are also helpful.

Most employers prefer to hire technicians who have completed a two-year training program in heating and cooling at a vocational or technical school. Another primary method of training is participation in a three- to five-year formal apprenticeship program.

Most heating and cooling technicians do not need a special license or certificate. A certificate is required, however, for technicians who handle potentially dangerous refrigerant materials such as Freon. Also, in some parts of the country there may be local requirements for certification.

To Be a Successful Heating and Cooling Technician, You Should . . .

○ have manual dexterity and an aptitude for working with tools

○ have the desire to perform challenging work that requires a high level of competence and quality

○ enjoy troubleshooting for mechanical and electrical problems

○ have strong communication skills

○ be willing to learn about new technology and systems throughout your career

Earnings

The earnings of heating and cooling technicians vary widely. Heating and cooling technicians had median hourly earnings of $18.11 (or $37,660 annually) in 2006, according to the U.S. Department of Labor. The lowest 10 percent earned less than $11.38 (or $23,680 annually), while the top 10 percent earned more than $28.57 (or $59,430 annually).

Heating and cooling apprentices usually earn about 50 percent of the wage rate paid to experienced workers. This percentage rises as apprentices gain experience and skill training in the field.

Outlook

Employment in the heating and cooling field is expected to increase faster than the average, according to the U.S. Department of Labor. Openings will occur when experienced workers retire or transfer to other work. Others will be generated because of a demand for new climate-control systems for residences and industrial and commercial users. In addition, many existing systems are being upgraded to provide more efficient use of energy and to provide benefits not originally built into the system.

Technicians who are involved in maintenance and repair are not as affected by the economy as workers in some other jobs. Whereas in bad economic times a consumer may put off building a new house or installing a new air-conditioning system, hospitals, restaurants, technical industries, and public buildings will still require skilled technicians to maintain their climate-control systems. Technicians who are skilled in more than one aspect of the job have greater job flexibility and can count on fairly steady work despite any changes in the economy.

FOR MORE INFO

For information on careers and educational programs, contact
Air Conditioning Contractors of America
2800 Shirlington Road, Suite 300
Arlington, VA 22206-3607
Tel: 703-575-4477
E-mail: info@acca.org
http://www.acca.org

For industry information, contact
American Society of Heating, Refrigerating and Air-Conditioning Engineers
1791 Tullie Circle N.E.
Atlanta, GA 30329
Tel: 404-636-8400
E-mail: ashrae@ashrae.org
http://www.ashrae.org

For industry information, contact
Plumbing-Heating-Cooling Contractors Association
180 South Washington Street
PO Box 6808
Falls Church, VA 22046-2900
Tel: 800-533-7694
E-mail: naphcc@naphcc.org
http://www.phccweb.org

Insulation Workers

What Insulation Workers Do

Insulation workers install building materials called insulation, which keeps hot or cold air in or out of a space. Insulation helps buildings to stay at the proper temperature and to ensure proper heating and cooling. Many different materials are used for insulation, including foam, fiberglass, insulating cements, cellulose, calcium silicate, or rock wool.

When insulating a wall, insulation workers may spray foam insulation onto crisscrossed wires called wire mesh. The foam sticks to the mesh and stays in place. Blown-in, loose-fill

Why Insulate?

Heat flows naturally from a warmer to a cooler space. In the winter, this heat flow moves directly from all heated living spaces to unheated attics, garages, and basements, or to the outdoors. To maintain comfort, the heat lost in winter must be replaced by a heating system and the heat gained in summer must be removed by an air conditioner.

Insulating ceilings, walls, and floors decreases this heat flow by providing an effective resistance to the flow of heat.

Inadequate insulation and air leakage are leading causes of energy waste in most homes. Insulation saves money and energy resources. Insulation can also act as a sound absorber or barrier, keeping noise levels down. The most important areas to insulate in a home are:

○ the attic, including the attic door, or hatch cover

○ under floors above unheated spaces, around walls in a heated basement or unventilated crawl space, and on the edges of slabs-on-grade

○ exterior walls for new house construction

A worker blows in fiberglass insulation to the attic space of a new home.
(David R. Frazier, The Image Works)

insulation includes loose fibers or fiber pellets that are blown into building cavities or attics using special pneumatic equipment. In some buildings, insulation workers staple *batts* or rolls of flexible insulation made from mineral fibers to parts of a building frame. To insulate a steam pipe, workers may slip the pipe into a tube-shaped length of insulation material. They may cover the insulation with an additional layer of metal to protect it from moisture. Rigid insulation is made from fibrous materials or plastic foams and is pressed or extruded into board-like forms and molded pipe coverings. Such boards may be faced with a reflective foil that reduces heat flow when next to an air space. Reflective insulation systems, made from aluminum foils with a variety of backings, are usually located between roof rafters, floor joists, or wall studs.

In major renovations or before the destruction of an old building, insulation workers must remove asbestos, an old type of insulation that has been discovered to cause cancer. Workers must follow special asbestos removal rules and practices. They must seal the area, then use special vacuum cleaners, air filters, and hand tools to remove the asbestos. Workers must also wear

EXPLORING

○ Ask your shop teacher to arrange a tour of a construction site to see an insulation worker at work.

○ Talk to an insulation worker about his or her career. Ask the following questions: What are your main and secondary job duties? What tools do you use to do your job? What are your typical work hours? What do you like least and most about your job? How did you train for this field? What advice would you give a young person who is interested in the field?

protective suits and respirators, and take a shower that decontaminates them when their work is done.

Education and Training

Insulation contractors usually prefer to hire individuals who have earned their high school diplomas and who have studied blueprint reading, mathematics, and sheet-metal and construction shop. If you are interested in becoming an insulation worker, you should take as many math and technical or shop courses as you can.

Most insulation workers learn their trade on the job. It usually takes about two years to learn professional insulation skills. Some people enter four-year apprenticeship programs that combine classroom instruction and practical insulation work. They must then pass an exam that includes both a written test and an insulation skill test. These

Mean Annual Earnings for Insulation Workers (Floor, Ceiling, and Wall) by Industry, 2006

Building equipment contractors:	$38,750
Nonresidential building construction:	$35,400
Foundation, structure, and building exterior contractors:	$34,820
Building finishing contractors:	$33,760
Other specialty trade contractors:	$33,700

Source: U.S. Department of Labor

programs are offered by local insulators and local branches of the International Association of Heat and Frost Insulators and Asbestos Workers, a labor union to which many insulation workers belong.

Earnings

In 2006, insulation workers earned about $17.25 an hour, according to the U.S. Department of Labor. Wages can range from less than $9.25 to $33.39 or more an hour. Insulation workers who do commercial and industrial work earn more than those who work in residential construction, which does not require as much skill.

Outlook

Job opportunities for insulation workers are expected to grow more slowly than the average due to the slowing growth of the construction industry (where many insulation workers are employed). Despite this prediction, the U.S. Department of Labor reports that employment opportunities are expected to be excellent. There is high turnover in this occupation, so there will continue to be a need for insulation workers in both new construction and in the renovation of older buildings. In addition, the growing focus on energy-efficient buildings will create additional opportunities for insulation workers.

FOR MORE INFO

For more information about training programs, contact the local branch of this union.
International Association of Heat and Frost Insulators and Asbestos Workers
602 M. L. King Jr. Highway
Lanham, MD 20706
Tel: 301-731-9101
http://www.insulators.org

For industry information, contact the following organizations.
Insulation Contractors Association of America
1321 Duke Street, Suite 303
Alexandria, VA 22314-3563
Tel: 703-739-0356
http://www.insulate.org

National Insulation Association
99 Canal Center Plaza, Suite 222
Alexandria, VA 22314-1588
Tel: 703-683-6422
http://www.insulation.org

Marble Setters, Tile Setters, and Terrazzo Workers

What Marble Setters, Tile Setters, and Terrazzo Workers Do

Marble, granite, and tiling have been used in the building trades for thousands of years. Many ancient temples were constructed of marble and granite and decorated with marble statues and beautifully colored tiles. Today, *marble setters, tile setters,* and *terrazzo workers* cover interior and exterior walls, floors, and other surfaces with marble, tile, and terrazzo.

These construction workers follow instructions from architects, builders, or homeowners. The materials they use—marble, tiles, terrazzo mixture, grout, mortar, and cement—are delivered

A Marble Masterpiece

The seventeenth-century Mogul emperor Shah Jahan had the Taj Mahal built in Agra, India, to house the remains of his beloved wife, Mumtaz Mahal.

Much of the Taj Mahal was made with pure marble. The basement, the dome, and the upper galleries of its minarets are inlaid with marble designs of different colors. Black marble letters spell out chapters of the Koran along the walls and passages. The tombs themselves are made of the purest marble inlaid with precious stones. They are surrounded by a marble screen six feet high, intricately carved with patterns of lilies, irises, and other flowers.

It is said that peace breathes from the Taj Mahal's stone. It has been called one of the great wonders of the world and one of the greatest works of art.

to the job site ready to be applied. In some cases, workers have to trim a piece of marble or cut tile to fit a particular space. Marble setters and tile setters are skilled at customizing such materials.

When setting marble, the workers first set out the pieces of marble to make sure that enough material has been delivered and that everything fits properly. Then the workers apply a special plaster to the marble and set the pieces in place. Grout, a sealing compound, is applied to the joints between the marble pieces. Finally, excess plaster and grout is polished away.

Tile setters use mortar or tile cement to apply tiles to horizontal or vertical surfaces. Some tiles are large—about a foot square or larger—and some are quite small—perhaps only an inch square. Smaller tiles often come in strips, attached to special backing material so that they do not have to be set individually.

Terrazzo workers create terrazzo by first laying a level base of concrete. On top of this base they pour a layer of concrete that has been mixed with marble or granite chips. These chips are usually brightly colored and may form a pattern or special hue. The wet concrete is rolled and leveled. In a few days, after both layers of concrete have hardened, workers use special grinding and polishing machines to finish the floor.

EXPLORING

○ The International Union of Brick-layers and Allied Craftworkers Web site (http://www.bacweb.org) has information on training and apprenticeship programs.
○ Try making a mosaic. Mosaics are constructed with many of the same processes as tile setting and terrazzo work, although on a much smaller scale.
○ Find an interesting construction site and watch workers and apprentices on their jobs.
○ Find out more about the International Masonry Institute's National Training Center in Bowie, Maryland. Once you become an apprentice, you could try to qualify for its 8- or 12-week program, which includes housing, food, and a nominal wage. Check its Web site (http://www.imiweb.org) for information on its National Terrazzo Training Program.

The Parthenon: Jobs for the Unemployed

Built in the fifth century B.C., the Parthenon is said to be one of the greatest buildings in the world. It is a marble structure more than 200 feet long and over 100 feet wide. Its surrounding columns are 34 feet tall. Marble for the building came from Mount Pentelikon, at least 10 miles away.

Workers cut blocks of marble from a quarry using mallets and chisels. They hammered wooden wedges into the marble and poured water over the blocks. The water caused the wood to swell, which in turn caused the marble to crack. Workers carried marble sections to the building site on oxcarts. At the site, skilled stone masons carved the marble into columns and blocks.

The Parthenon is said to have contributed to creating jobs. The Persian Wars had just ended, leaving soldiers unemployed. Unskilled laborers, including the soldiers, were hired to level the ground, inspect the marble blocks, and drag stone up the slopes of the Acropolis, the hill upon which the Parthenon is built.

Education and Training

Marble setters, tile setters, and terrazzo workers are building trade workers as well as craftworkers. If you wish to pursue a career in one of these trades you need a high school diploma and you must be at least 17 years old. High school courses that are helpful include art, blueprint reading, math, and any shop courses that will train you to use hand tools.

After high school, you can become an apprentice to a marble setter, tile setter, or terrazzo worker through either a union or an individual building contractor. An apprenticeship program usually consists of about 6,000 hours, or three years, of a combination of classroom instruction and on-the-job training.

Earnings

According to the U.S. Department of Labor, median hourly earnings of tile and marble setters were $17.59 (or $36,590 annually) in 2006. Wages ranged from less than $10.26 (or $21,330 annually) to more than $29.95 an hour (or $62,290 annually). Terrazzo workers earned salaries that ranged from less than $19,360 to $56,610 or more in 2006, according to the U.S. Department of Labor. Earnings of marble setters, tile setters, and terrazzo workers vary by union membership and geographic location. The highest wages are paid in urban areas. Wages vary at different geographic locations throughout the United States, with the highest rates paid in cities. Apprentices start by earning about half of what the skilled worker earns, but they earn more as they learn more.

Outlook

Employment for tile and marble setters is expected to grow about as fast as the average, according to the U.S. Department of Labor. Job opportunities for tile setters will not be as plentiful as in other construction occupations because the field is small and turnover is low. Tile is expected to continue to increase in popularity as a building material and to be used more extensively, particularly in more expensive homes, whose construction is expected to increase. Workers may find that work is steadier in warmer climates. Terrazzo is popular in warm, southwestern states like California and Texas, as well as in Florida.

FOR MORE INFO

For information on apprenticeships and other training opportunities, contact
International Masonry Institute
The James Brice House
42 East Street
Annapolis, MD 21401-1731
Tel: 410-280-1305
E-mail: imitraining@imiweb.org
http://imiweb.org

For information on training and employment, contact
International Union of Bricklayers and Allied Craftworkers
620 F Street NW
Washington, DC 20004-1618
Tel: 888-880-8222
E-mail: askbac@bacweb.org
http//www.bacweb.org

For information on national standards and continuing educational seminars, contact
National Terrazzo and Mosaic Association
201 North Maple, Suite 208
Purcellville, VA 20132-6102
Tel: 800-323-9736
E-mail: info@ntma.com
http://www.ntma.com

Operating Engineers

What Operating Engineers Do

Operating engineers operate large machines used in digging, grading, moving, lifting, and similar activities on construction projects.

Many operating engineers work for companies that build highways, dams, airports, and other large-scale projects. Others are employed by contractors who construct residential or commercial buildings. Utility companies, big manufacturing companies, and other businesses that do their own construction work, including mines and steel mills, also need operating engineers to run heavy equipment. States, cities, and towns hire operating engineers as part of construction and repair crews in their highway and public works departments.

Operating engineers must have excellent mechanical aptitude and skillful coordination of eye, hand, and foot movements. (Construction Photography, Corbis)

Whatever employer they work for, operating engineers run power shovels, cranes, derricks, hoists, pile drivers, concrete mixers, paving machines, bulldozers, tractors, and pumps. In many instances, operators do this sitting in a cab compartment of the machine and using pedals, levers, switches, and dials located on a control panel.

Operating engineers are often known by the type of machine they operate. *Bulldozer operators,* for example, drive bulldozers and raise and lower the blade to move rocks, trees, earth, or other obstacles from a construction site. *Crane operators* rotate the crane on its chassis or raise or lower the boom. They must be able to use various attachments to the boom, such as buckets, pile drivers, or heavy wrecking balls. *Hoist and winch operators* lift and pull heavy loads using power-operated equipment. Many operating engineers are qualified to operate more than one type of machine, and they may operate and maintain compressors, pumps, and other power equipment at the work site.

EXPLORING

○ Read books and magazines about power shovels, cranes, concrete mixers, paving machines, bulldozers, tractors, and other heavy machinery.

○ Talk to an operating engineer about his or her career. Ask the following questions: What are your main and secondary job duties? What do you like least and most about your job? How did you train for this field? What advice would you give a young person who is interested in the field?

○ Once you get into high school, try to get a summer job as a laborer or machine operator's helper in a construction job. Such jobs may be available on local, state, and federal highway and building construction programs.

Education and Training

Most employers prefer to hire operating engineers who are high school graduates. Classes in automobile mechanics are good preparation for this field. Often, employers look for operating engineers who have been trained in a three-year apprenticeship program after high school. Apprenticeship programs combine classroom instruction with on-the-job training on a

To Be a Successful Operating Engineer, You Should . . .

○ have excellent mechanical aptitude

○ have good coordination of eye, hand, and foot movements

○ be responsible and careful when working with potentially dangerous machinery

○ have strong communication skills

○ be in good health

○ be able to deal with loud and dirty working conditions

wide variety of machines. Operating engineers can also get training through private vocational schools.

Earnings

The median annual salary for all operating engineers and other construction equipment operators was approximately $36,890 in 2006, according to the U.S. Department of Labor. Salaries ranged from less than $24,010 to more than $64,120 a year. Rates vary according to the area of the country and the type of employer. In highway, street, and bridge construction, the mean salary was $44,420 in 2006. Those working in heavy construction (except highway work) earned $41,170. Rates also vary by the type of machine being operated. Crane and tower operators earned a median annual salary of $39,040 in 2006. Excavation and loading machine operators earned $32,930 a year. Hoist and winch operators earned $33,620.

Outlook

Employment of operating engineers working in the construction industry is projected to grow about as fast as the average, according to the U.S. Department of Labor. Although job growth will be somewhat limited by increased efficiency

How Did They Do That?

Scientists and engineers still puzzle over the system that ancient Egyptians used to move the giant stone blocks of the pyramids into place. The Romans constructed roads, viaducts, and bridges of high quality, many of which are still in use today. The Great Wall of China, begun in the third century B.C., remains an amazing architectural feat.

These ancient marvels of engineering are even more amazing when you consider that they were all built using only human muscle and simple machines such as levers and pulleys. It was not until the Industrial Revolution and the invention of the steam engine that complex machines were extensively used in construction. After the harnessing of steam power, western Europe and America made rapid progress in constructing buildings, roads, and water and sewage systems.

brought about by automation, there will be many opportunities for operating engineers. About 60 percent of operating engineers work in construction and local government—industries that are associated with the construction and repair of highways, bridges, dams, harbors, airports, subways, water and sewage systems, power plants, and transmission lines.

FOR MORE INFO

Contact the following organizations for further information about a career as an operating engineer.

Associated General Contractors of America
2300 Wilson Boulevard, Suite 400
Arlington, VA 22201-5426
Tel: 703-548-3118
E-mail: info@agc.org
http://www.agc.org

International Union of Operating Engineers
1125 17th Street NW
Washington, DC 20036-4707
Tel: 202-429-9100
http://www.iuoe.org

Painters and Paperhangers

What Painters and Paperhangers Do

Painters apply paint, stain, varnish, and other finishes to buildings and other structures. *Paperhangers* cover walls and ceilings with decorative wall coverings made of paper, vinyl, or fabric. Workers in the painting and paperhanging trades often perform both functions.

Painters know how to use brushes and other painting tools and understand the characteristics of various paints and finishes. When repainting old surfaces, painters remove old, loose paint, and fill nail holes, cracks, and joints with putty, plaster, or other types of filler.

Once the surface is prepared, painters select premixed paints or prepare paint. They apply the paint with brushes, spray guns, or rollers. Choosing the best tool for applying paint

What Is Paint?

Liquid paints have two main parts—a pigment and a vehicle. *Pigments* are finely ground powders that give the paint color and opacity (hiding power). *Vehicles* are liquids that act as a base for the pigment. They consist of binders and solvents. *Binders* hold the paint film together and make it stick to a surface. *Solvents,* also called *thinners,* are substances that reduce the paint's consistency so it can be applied or removed easily.

To make paint, pigment is mixed with a small amount of binder. The mixture is ground in a mill until a smooth paste forms. The paste is then mixed with the solvent and additional binder. Most paint stores have mixing machines that can create a wide range of colors, tints, and shades from the basic colors prepared at the paint factory. Professional painters often prefer to mix their own paints on the job.

All About Wallpaper

Wallpaper is usually printed with a colored pattern or design. Wallpaper for bathrooms and kitchens is often made of paper or fabric covered with plastic. Plastic-covered fabrics are sometimes called wall coverings. Wallpaper is hung by means of an adhesive. With ordinary wallpaper, a paste is brushed onto the back of the paper before it is hung. Prepasted wallpapers are also available. With some prepasted wallpapers, the adhesive must be moistened with water before hanging. Others are ready to be hung when a protective backing is peeled off. There are special wallpapers made so that they can be easily removed when redecorating is desired. Ordinary wallpaper usually must be steamed to loosen the old adhesive.

The most expensive grades of wallpaper are block printed by hand or printed by the silk-screen process. They may be made in panels or in long rolls. Less expensive wallpaper and wall coverings are made and printed by mass-production methods. Flock papers, which imitate tapestries, are made by printing the design in size (a glue-like material) and then covering the wet size with ground wool, sill, or other fibers of various colors.

is important because the wrong tool can slow down work on a job and produce unacceptable results.

Many painters specialize in working on exterior surfaces, such as house sidings and outside walls of large buildings. When painting tall structures, painters stand on ladders or scaffolding (raised supportive platforms).

Paperhangers also have to prepare surfaces. They smooth rough spots, fill holes and cracks, and remove old paint and varnish. In some cases, old wallpaper must be removed. Paperhangers first apply sizing to surfaces, which ensures that the paper will adhere well.

Paperhangers measure the area to be covered and cut the paper to size. They mix paste and apply it to the back of the paper, which they place on the wall or ceiling and smooth into place with brushes or rollers. In placing the paper on the wall, paperhangers make sure that they match any design patterns exactly.

EXPLORING

○ Read trade publications about the field, such as the *Painters and Allied Trades Journal* (http://www.iupat.org/about/publications.html).

○ Offer your help to family or neighbors who are redecorating their homes.

○ Watch instructional videos, DVDs, or television programs about home construction and renovation.

○ Talk to a painter about his or her career. Ask the following questions: What are your main and secondary job duties? What tools do you use to do your job? What are your typical work hours? What do you like least and most about your job? How did you train for this field? What advice would you give a young person who is interested in the field?

Painters and paperhangers take safety precautions to avoid breathing noxious fumes and dust. There are also safety concerns in using ladders or scaffolding. Painters and paperhangers have to stand for long periods and do a lot of climbing, reaching, and bending.

Education and Training

Most painting contractors like to hire workers who are in good physical condition, work well with their hands, and have a good sense of color. Employers also prefer workers who have a high school diploma. Shop classes can help prepare you for the manual work involved in painting and paperhanging, while art classes will help develop an eye for color and design.

To become a skilled painter or paperhanger, you must finish either an apprenticeship program or on-the-job training. Apprenticeship programs take about three years and include both work experience and classroom study. While this kind of instruction is very helpful, painters and paperhangers can, in general, enter the profession by training on the job with experienced workers.

Earnings

Painters and paperhangers tend to earn more per hour than many other construction workers, but their total annual incomes may be less because of work time lost due to poor weather and periods of layoffs between contract assignments. In 2006, median hourly earnings of painters in construction and maintenance were $15.00 (or $31,190 annually), according to the

To Be a Successful Painter and Paperhanger, You Should . . .

- ○ be in good physical health
- ○ have excellent manual dexterity and a good sense of color
- ○ not be allergic to paint fumes or other materials used in the trade
- ○ be willing to perform sometimes repetitive tasks
- ○ be attentive to detail
- ○ be willing to work in all types of weather conditions

U.S. Department of Labor. Hourly wages ranged from less than $9.97 (or $20,740 annually) to more than $25.62 (or $53,280 annually). The USDL reports that paperhangers earned a median hourly salary of $16.21 (or $33,710 annually) in 2006. Hourly wage rates for apprentices usually start at 40 to 50 percent of the rate for experienced workers and increase periodically.

Outlook

Job opportunities for painters and paperhangers depend largely on growth in the construction industry, although there will always be opportunities for painters to work on remodeling, restoration, and maintenance projects. The U.S. Department of Labor predicts that jobs will grow about as fast as the average. Turnover is very high in this trade, so most job openings occur when other workers change occupations. There will be fewer jobs for paperhangers than for painters because it is a smaller, specialized trade.

FOR MORE INFO

For career and training information for painters, contact the following organizations.

International Union of Painters and Allied Trades
1750 New York Avenue NW
Washington, DC 20006-5301
Tel: 202-637-0700
E-mail: mail@iupat.org
http://www.iupat.org

Painting and Decorating Contractors of America
1801 Park 270 Drive, Suite 220
St. Louis, MO 63146-4020
Tel: 800-332-7322
http://www.pdca.org

Plasterers

What Plasterers Do

Plastering is one of the original crafts in the building trades. *Plasterers* apply coats of plaster to the walls and ceilings inside buildings. Plaster produces a fire-resistant and somewhat soundproof surface. Plasterers also work on the exteriors of buildings, applying a type of plaster known as stucco or a type of exterior insulation made of acrylic, styrofoam, and chemicals. Some plasterers do ornamental forming and casting work to create intricate building decorations out of plaster.

Plasterers apply plaster directly to masonry, wire mesh, wood, or lath, which is a supportive reinforcement made

Words to Learn

aggregate an ingredient of plaster, such as sand, pumice, or vermiculite, that keeps it from shrinking while it sets and to add bulk

binder an ingredient of plaster that holds it together and makes it stick; common binders are slaked lime and gypsum

brown coat the second coat of a three-coat work; it creates an even surface

finish coat a very thin, final coat of fine white plaster; in machine application, the plaster is sprayed onto the surface

hawk a flat board with a handle that the plasterer uses to hold wet plaster

lath a support made of wire mesh, open-work metal, gypsum board, or wood slats

scratch coat The first coat in a three-coat work; the scratch coat is pressed firmly to the lath with a trowel and then roughened with a tool called a *scarifier*

of wood, gypsum board, and metal. First, plasterers apply a border of plaster around the edges of a surface. When the border has hardened, the rest of the surface is filled in with plaster. Usually, two coats of plaster are used during this stage. Plasterers then smooth the surface and level it. Finally, they apply a third coat of plaster. They finish this coat to a satin smoothness so that it can be painted or covered with wallpaper.

Sometimes, plasterers work with wallboard, which is made up of prefinished sheets of plaster. Plasterers cut the wallboard to the desired height and width, and then attach it to ceilings and interior walls. This is a much faster method of plastering than applying wet plaster in coats.

Plasterers who work on exterior walls are sometimes called *stucco masons*. Stucco masons apply a decorative coat of plaster that consists of white cement and sand. This type of plaster is weather resistant. It is mixed in many different colors and textures, and is often applied with a spray gun.

Molding plasterers create decorated plaster shapes. For example, a doorway may have a frame around it that looks like hand-carved wood but is actually made of molded plaster.

EXPLORING

○ Learn more about plasterers by reading books and magazines and surfing the Internet.
○ Take mechanical drawing, drafting, woodwork, and other shop courses in school. Art classes, especially sculpture, might also give you the chance to work with plaster and plaster mixtures and molds.
○ Take a field trip to a construction site to observe a plasterer at work.
○ Talk to a plasterer about his or her career. Ask the following questions: What type of tools do you use in your job? What are your typical work hours? What do you like least and most about your job? How did you train for this field? What advice would you give a young person who is interested in the field?

Education and Training

Employers prefer to hire workers who have at least a high school diploma and are in good physical condition.

Plaster Project

Here is a project to help you get a feel for plaster and its properties. You'll need:

- vermiculite (available at hardware stores and places that sell gardening supplies)
- plaster of paris
- water
- container for mixing
- rubber gloves
- cardboard box, milk carton, styrofoam cup, or plastic bowl
- modeling tools (a butter knife, fork, spoon, nail, or other household items)
- sandpaper

Mix one part vermiculite with one part plaster of paris. Add one to two parts water until the mixture is the consistency of cake batter. Mix with your hands until you get all the lumps out. Pour the mixture into your milk carton or other container. Tap the side of the container to let the air bubbles come to the top. Let it harden. After it hardens, carefully remove the mold. Now you're ready to begin carving designs into the plaster mixture or create a small sculpture. If you don't finish your carving in one sitting, you can keep it moist by covering it with a plastic bag. If you are happy with your work, you can seal it with acrylic sealer.

You can experiment with the recipe, too. Mixing two parts plaster with three parts vermiculite will give you a much softer material. Mixing two parts plaster with one part vermiculite will give a harder material.

Apprenticeships are a standard training method. You must be at least 17 years old to enter an apprenticeship program. The program consists of two to three years of carefully supervised

Mean Annual Earnings for Plasterers by Industry, 2006

Nonresidential building construction:	$43,340
Building finishing contractors:	$38,190
Residential building construction:	$36,480
Foundation, structure, and building exterior contractors:	$33,320
Other specialty trade contractors:	$33,000

Source: U.S. Department of Labor

on-the-job experience and classroom instruction. At the end of the apprenticeship program, the apprentice becomes a journeyman plasterer.

Earnings

Plasterers earned median annual salaries of $34,700 in 2006, according to the U.S. Department of Labor. Earnings ranged from less than $22,540 to more than $56,810. Plasterers in New York, Boston, Chicago, San Francisco, Los Angeles, and other large cities received the highest hourly earnings. Starting pay for apprentices is about 50 percent of a journeyman plasterer's wage and increases as they gain experience.

Outlook

Employment of plasterers should grow more slowly than the average, according to the U.S. Department of Labor. Despite this prediction, opportunities should be good as workers leave the field for less physically demanding jobs or for other reasons. In past years, employment of plasterers declined as more builders switched to drywall construction. This decline has halted, however, and employment of plasterers is expected to continue growing because of the durability and attractiveness of its troweled finishes.

FOR MORE INFO

For information on education in the wall and ceiling industry, contact
Association of the Wall and Ceiling Industry
513 West Broad Street,
Suite 210
Falls Church, VA 22046-3257
Tel: 703-538-1600
http://www.awci.org

For information on the lath and plaster industry, contact
International Institute for Lath and Plaster
Lath & Plaster Information Bureau
PO Box 3922
Palm Desert, CA 92260-3922
Tel: 760-837-9094
http://www.iilp.org

For information about construction trades, training, and union membership, contact
International Union of Bricklayers and Allied Craftworkers
620 F Street NW
Washington, DC 20004-1618
Tel: 888-880-8222
E-mail: askbac@bacweb.org
http://www.bacweb.org

For information on membership and apprenticeships, contact
Operative Plasterers' and Cement Masons' International Association
11720 Beltsville Drive, Suite 700
Beltsville, MD 20705-3104
Tel: 301-623-1000
E-mail: opcmiaintl@opcmia.org
http://www.opcmia.org

Plumbers

What Plumbers Do

Plumbers install and repair water, drainage, waste, and ventilation systems in homes and commercial buildings. They also install fixtures such as sinks and toilets, and appliances such as washing machines. Plumbers may fix broken or rusted pipes and repair bathtubs, garbage disposals, water heaters, and dishwashers. They sometimes install or service septic tanks, cesspools, and sewers.

When a new building is under construction, plumbers are part of the construction team. They work from blueprints or drawings that show the planned location of pipes, plumbing fixtures, and appliances. They lay out the job to fit the piping into the structure. They measure and mark areas where pipes will be installed and connected. Before the walls are completed, they install water pipes and heating and air-conditioning units. They also connect radiators, water heaters, and plumbing fixtures.

Once plumbers know what size a pipe has to be, they cut it and bend it to the proper angle. They join pipe pieces by welding, caulking, or screwing them together. To test for leaks, they fill the pipes with air or water and look for problem spots.

Plumbers use a number of tools in their work. These include wrenches, drills, hammers, chisels, power machines for cutting and bending metal, and torches and other welding equipment.

Plumbing Problems

○ Flooding may be caused by a broken pipe, or, more commonly, by a backed-up sewer.

○ Leaks most often occur because of worn washers in faucets or an improperly adjusted float in a toilet tank.

○ Clogged drains are usually the result of an accumulation of hair or grease.

○ Frozen pipes can cause flooding when they finally thaw. Since water expands when it freezes, the expansion may burst the pipes.

EXPLORING

○ Learn more about plumbers by reading books and magazines and surfing the Internet.

○ If possible, have a parent or family member show you how to do minor plumbing repairs, such as fixing a running toilet or replacing worn-out washers.

○ Talk to a plumber about his or her career. Ask the following questions: What do you like least and most about your job? How did you train for this field? What advice would you give a young person who is interested in the field?

Did You Know?

○ The word "plumbing" comes from the Latin *plumbum*, meaning "lead," the material formerly used to make pipes. Modern pipes are made of copper, galvanized iron or steel, cast iron, brass, or plastic.

○ Plumbers and pipefitters held about 561,000 jobs in 2004. About 50 percent worked for mechanical and plumbing contractors engaged in new construction, repair, modernization, or maintenance work.

Plumbers usually work a 40-hour week, with extra pay for overtime. Unlike other construction industry jobs, plumbing work is available all year round. Plumbing is physically active and strenuous work.

Education and Training

There are two ways to become a plumber. One is to become an apprentice and the other is to train on the job. To become an apprentice, you must first apply to an apprenticeship committee. Local plumbing contractors, plumbers' unions, or state employment bureaus can provide information on where and how to apply. Apprentices train with experienced plumbers on the job to learn their trade. After learning all the necessary skills, apprentices become journeymen plumbers. Those who are not accepted into apprenticeship programs can learn to be plumbers by working for others and learning on the job.

Many plumbers go into business for themselves. Some become plumbing contractors and employ other plumbers.

Earnings

The median hourly salary for plumbers who were not self-employed was $20.56 in 2006, according to the U.S. Department of Labor. Wages range from $12.30 to $34.79 an hour and vary according to location. Plumbers

The Plumber's Apprentice

An apprenticeship offers four to five years of on-the-job training in addition to at least 144 hours a year of classroom work. Classroom subjects include drafting and blueprint reading, mathematics, applied physics and chemistry, and local plumbing codes and regulations. On the job, apprentices first learn how to identify grades and types of pipe, use the tools of the trade, and safely unload materials. They learn how to work with various types of pipe and how to install different piping systems and plumbing fixtures until they develop a thorough knowledge of all aspects of the trade.

employed in nonresidential construction had mean salaries of $46,580, while those employed in utility system construction earned $42,500. Hourly pay rates for apprentices usually start at 50 percent of the experienced worker's rate and increase by 5 percent every six months until a rate of 95 percent is reached.

Outlook

Employment for plumbers is expected to grow about as fast as the average, according to the U.S. Department of Labor. The department predicts excellent opportunities for plumbers due to a shortage of workers entering the field and a projected wave of retirements in the next decade. Construction activity is expected to grow slowly, and more plumbers will find work in renovation, repair, and maintenance. Since pipework is becoming more important in large industries, more workers will be needed for installation and maintenance work, especially where refrigeration and air-conditioning equipment are used.

FOR MORE INFO

For more information about becoming a plumber, contact the following organizations.

Plumbing-Heating-Cooling Contractors Association
180 South Washington Street
PO Box 6808
Falls Church, VA 22046-2900
Tel: 800-533-7694
E-mail: naphcc@naphcc.org
http://www.phccweb.org

United Association of Journeymen and Apprentices of the Plumbing and Pipe Fitting Industry of the United States and Canada
901 Massachusetts Avenue NW
Washington, DC 20001-4397
Tel: 202-628-5823
http://www.ua.org

Roofers

What Roofers Do

Roofers apply roofing materials, including tile and slate shingles, to the roofs of buildings. They also waterproof and damp-proof walls, swimming pools, and other building surfaces. Although roofers usually are trained to apply most kinds of roofing, they often specialize in either sheet membrane roofing or prepared roofing such as asphalt shingles, slate, or tile.

The most common type of roofing is composition roofing. In one type of composition roofing, called built-up roofing, roofers place overlapping strips of asphalt or tar-coated felt to the roof. Then they spread a thin layer of hot asphalt or coal tar pitch over the felt strips. The roofers continue alternating felt strips and hot

Parts of a Roof

deck the surface attached to the support frame to which roofing is applied

dormer a framed window unit that projects through the sloping plane of a roof

eave the horizontal, lower edge of a sloped roof

flashing pieces of metal or roll roofing that prevent water leaking in around vent pipes, chimneys, adjoining walls, dormers, or valleys

gable the top portion of a sidewall that comes to a triangular point where it meets the ridge of a sloping roof

rake the inclined edge of a sloped roof over a wall from the eave to the ridge

ridge the uppermost horizontal angle formed by the intersection of two sloping roof planes

vent any outlet for air that sticks through the roof deck, such as a pipe or stack

asphalt or pitch until they reach the desired thickness. Finally, a top coat of coal tar pitch and gravel or a smooth coat of asphalt is applied. On some composition roofs, asphalt shingles or rolls of roofing material are affixed with nails or asphalt cement.

Another type of composition roofing is single-ply roofing. Single-ply roofs differ from built-up roofs in the way their seams are sealed: contact adhesive cements, hot-air welders, solvent welding, and propane or butane torches are used. Many manufacturers of these systems require that roofers take special courses and receive certification before they are allowed to use the products.

Tile and slate shingles, which are more expensive types of residential roofing, are installed a little differently. First, roofing felt is applied over the wood base. Next, the roofers punch holes in the slate or tile pieces so that nails can be inserted, or they embed the tiles in mortar. Each row of shingles overlaps the preceding row.

Metal roofing is applied by roofers or by sheet metal workers. One type of metal roof uses metal sections shaped like flat pans, soldered together for weather-proofing and attached by metal clips to the wood below. Standing seam roofing has

What Are Shingles?

A *shingle* is a small, thin, flat or tapering piece of material used to surface roofs or exterior walls. Most shingles are made of composite material. Asphalt singles, for example, consist of roofing felt saturated with asphalt and covered with small pebbles on the exterior. Shingles are usually nailed in place in an overlapping pattern. The amount of overlapping depends on the angle of the surface—the steeper the surface, the less overlapping is required.

Wood shingles are sometimes used, chiefly for decorative effects. *Shakes* are shingles that have been split from a piece of wood and show a rough, raised grain pattern, while ordinary wood shingles are relatively smooth. Cedar is a common wood for shingles and shakes.

EXPLORING

○ Learn more about roofers by reading books and magazines and surfing the Internet.

○ It may be possible to visit a construction site to observe roofers at work, but a close look is unlikely as roofers do most of their work at heights.

○ High school or vocational school students may be able to get first-hand experience of this occupation through a part-time or summer job as a roofer's helper.

raised seams where the sections of sheet metal interlock.

Roofers may waterproof and damp-proof structures other than roofs. First, the roofers smooth rough surfaces and slightly roughen glazed surfaces. Next, they apply waterproofing fabric to the surface, either with a brush or by spraying. Damp-proofing, which prevents moisture from penetrating building surfaces, is done by spraying a coat of tar or asphalt onto the building surfaces.

Education and Training

Employers prefer to hire applicants who are at least 18 years old and who have earned a high school diploma. Roofers must complete an apprenticeship or on-the-job training program. Apprenticeships usually last for three years and on-the-job training lasts four or five years.

To Be a Successful Roofer, You Should . . .

○ not be afraid of heights

○ have a good sense of balance

○ have good hand-eye coordination

○ be attentive to detail because this job can sometimes be dangerous

○ be able to follow directions

○ enjoy working outdoors

○ be able to work as a member of a team

○ have strong communication and mathematical skills

Earnings

In 2006, median hourly earnings of roofers were $15.51, according to the U.S. Department of Labor. Wages ranged from less than $9.81 to more than $26.79. Layoffs during bad weather limit the number of hours roofers work. Hourly rates for apprentices usually start at about 40 to 50 percent of the skilled worker's rate and their earnings gradually increase during the training period.

Outlook

Employment for roofers is expected to increase about as fast as the average, according to the U.S. Department of Labor. Roofs tend to need more maintenance work than other parts of buildings, so roofers will always be needed for repairs and replacement. About 75 percent of roofing work is on existing structures. Also, damp-proofing and waterproofing are expected to provide more jobs for roofers. Turnover in this job is high because roofing work is strenuous, hot, and dirty. Many workers consider roofing a temporary job and move into other construction trades. Since roofing is done during the warmer part of the year, job opportunities will probably be best during spring and summer.

FOR MORE INFO

This organization offers plenty of information and membership benefits to professional roofers, including a magazine.

National Roofing Contractors Association
10255 West Higgins Road, Suite 600
Rosemont, IL 60018-5607
Tel: 847-299-9070
http://www.nrca.net

This union's Web site has information on careers in roofing.

United Union of Roofers, Waterproofers, and Allied Workers
1660 L Street NW, Suite 800
Washington, DC 20036-5646
Tel: 202-463-7663
E-mail: roofers@unionroofers.com
http://www.unionroofers.com

Welders

What Welders Do

Welders join metal pieces together by applying heat, pressure, or both, until the edges of the metals meet and the pieces are permanently fused. This process is used in the manufacturing and repair of thousands of different products, from water faucets and refrigerators to cars, airplanes, and missiles. There are more than 80 different welding processes.

Fusion welding joins the welded parts by heat alone. The parts are heated until they melt and flow together. Any space left between the two parts is filled with metal from a welding rod of the same composition as the metal being welded. In arc welding, one kind of fusion welding, the worker strikes an arc (creates an electric current) by touching the metal with an electrode. An electrode is a type of tool (usually made of metal) that conducts electric current. The welder guides the electrode along the metal seams until the heat of the arc melts the metal. Another type of fusion welding is gas welding. Heat is supplied by gases burned in a torch. The hot flame melts both the parts to be welded and the welding rod.

Resistance welding and flash welding are two types of plastic welding.

Welders need manual dexterity, good eye-hand coordination, and good eyesight, as well as patience and the ability to concentrate for extended periods as they work on a task. (Michael Wickes, The Image Works)

Plastic welding is done by heating the parts until they soften, and then joining them by pressure. Resistance welding is used to join thin sheets of metal. In flash welding, the parts to be welded are brought together, edge to edge, in a hydraulic press. An electric arc appears between the edges as they are brought near each other. When the arc has softened the metal, the two edges are abruptly squeezed together.

Working conditions for welders are often considered potentially hazardous. They wear protective clothing, goggles, hard hats, and other gear to avoid burns and injuries. Also, because some metals give off toxic gases as they are melted, the work area must always be properly ventilated.

EXPLORING

○ Learn more about welding careers by reading books and magazines and surfing the Internet.
○ Ask your teacher or guidance counselor to arrange to visit a workplace where you can observe welders or welding machine operators on the job.

Welding Pros and Cons

Pros:

○ Welding provides a permanent joint. The welded parts become a single entity.
○ A welded joint can be stronger than the parent materials.
○ Welding is usually the most economical way to join components in terms of materials costs.
○ Welding doesn't have to be done in a factory. It can be done in the field.

Cons:

○ Manual welding operations are expensive in terms of labor cost. Skilled labor may be scarce.
○ Most welding processes are dangerous.
○ Since welding forms a permanent bond between the parts, it is difficult to undo a weld.
○ The welded joint can have quality defects that are difficult to detect. The defects can reduce the strength of the joint.

FOR MORE INFO

For more information about a career in welding, contact
American Welding Society
550 NW LeJeune Road
Miami, FL 33126
Tel: 800-443-9353
E-mail: info@aws.org
http://www.aws.org

For information on union membership, contact
International Association of Machinists and Aerospace Workers
9000 Machinists Place
Upper Marlboro, MD 20772-2687
Tel: 301-967-4500
E-mail: websteward@iamaw.org
http://www.iamaw.org

Education and Training

For skilled welding jobs (where workers travel to construction sites or utility plants to do repairs), employers prefer to hire welders with a high school or vocational school diploma.

Many welders learn their skills in formal training programs offered at community colleges, at trade schools, and in the armed forces. Beginners can also learn welding skills in on-the-job training programs. The length of training time varies from several weeks for jobs requiring few skills to between one and three years for more skilled jobs.

Apprenticeship programs that teach a range of metalworking skills, including the basics of welding, are offered by trade unions, such as the International Association of Machinists and Aerospace Workers.

Earnings

The U.S. Department of Labor reports that median annual earnings of welders in 2006 were $31,400. Salaries ranged from less than $20,970 to $46,800 or more.

Outlook

Overall employment in welding is expected to grow more slowly than average, according to the U.S. Department of Labor. Despite the slow growth, there should be plenty of opportunities for skilled welders, since many employers have difficulties in finding qualified applicants. The outlook varies by industry. Opportunities will be best in construction and weakest in manufacturing.

Glossary

accredited approved as meeting established standards for providing good training and education; this approval is usually given by an independent organization of professionals

apprentice a person who is learning a trade by working under the supervision of a skilled worker; apprentices often receive classroom instruction in addition to their supervised practical experience

associate's degree an academic rank or title granted by a community or junior college or similar institution to graduates of a two-year program of education beyond high school

bachelor's degree an academic rank or title given to a person who has completed a four-year program of study at a college or university; also called an undergraduate degree or baccalaureate

career an occupation for which a worker receives training and has an opportunity for advancement

certified approved as meeting established requirements for skill, knowledge, and experience in a particular field; people are certified by the organization of professionals in their field

college a higher education institution that is above the high school level

community college a public or private two-year college attended by students who do not usually live at the college; graduates of a community college receive an associate's degree and may transfer to a four-year college or university to complete a bachelor's degree

diploma a certificate or document given by a school to show that a person has completed a course or has graduated from the school

distance education a type of educational program that allows students to take classes and complete their education by mail or the Internet

doctorate the highest academic rank or title granted by a graduate school to a person who has completed a program after having received a master's degree

fringe benefit a payment or benefit to an employee in addition to regular wages or salary; examples of fringe benefits include a pension, a paid vacation, and health or life insurance

graduate school a school that people may attend after they have received their bachelor's degree; people who complete an educational program at a graduate school earn a master's degree or a doctorate

intern an advanced student (usually one with at least some college training) in a professional field who is employed in a job that is intended to provide supervised practical experience for the student

internship (1) The position or job of an intern; (2) the period of time when a person is an intern

junior college a two-year college that offers courses like those in the first half of a four-year college program; graduates of a junior college usually receive an associate's degree and may transfer to a four-year college or university to complete a bachelor's degree

liberal arts the subjects covered by college courses that develop broad general knowledge rather than specific occupational skills; the liberal arts often include philosophy, literature and the arts, history, language, and some courses in the social sciences and natural sciences

licensed having formal permission from the proper authority to carry out an activity that would be illegal without that permission;

for example, a person must be licensed to practice medicine or drive a car

major the academic field in which a college student specializes and receives a degree

master's degree an academic rank or title granted by a graduate school to a person who has completed a program after having received a bachelor's degree

pension an amount of money paid regularly by an employer to a former employee after he or she retires from working

scholarship a gift of money to a student to help the student pay for further education

social studies courses of study (such as civics, geography, and history) that deal with how human societies work

starting salary salary paid to a newly hired employee; the starting salary is usually a smaller amount than is paid to a more experienced worker

technical college a private or public college offering two- or four-year programs in technical subjects; technical colleges offer courses in both general and technical subjects and award associate's degrees and bachelor's degrees

technician a worker with specialized practical training in a mechanical or scientific subject who works under the supervision of scientists, engineers, or other professionals; technicians typically receive two years of college-level education after high school

technologist a worker in a mechanical or scientific field with more training than a technician; technologists typically must have between two and four years of college-level education after high school

undergraduate a student at a college or university who has not yet received a degree

undergraduate degree see **bachelor's degree**

union an organization whose members are workers in a particular industry or company; the union works to gain better wages, benefits, and working conditions for its members; also called a labor union or trade union

vocational school a public or private school that offers training in one or more skills or trades

wage money that is paid in return for work done, especially money paid on the basis of the number of hours or days worked

Index of Job Titles

Browse and Learn More

Books

Frew, Katherine. *Plumber.* New York: Children's Press, 2004.

Haddock, Keith. *Colossal Earthmovers.* Osceola, Wisc.: Motorbooks International, 2000.

Haycraft, William R. *Yellow Steel: The Story of the Earthmoving Equipment Industry.* Champaign, Ill.: University of Illinois Press, 2002.

Jefferis, David. *Extreme Structures: Mega-Constructions of the 21st Century.* New York: Crabtree Publishing Company, 2006.

O'Connor, Rachel. *Construction Worker.* New York: Children's Press, 2004.

Orlemann, Eric. *Caterpillar Chronicle: The History of the World's Greatest Earth Movers.* Osceola, Wisc.: Motorbooks International, 2000.

Overcamp, David. *Electrician.* New York: Children's Press, 2004.

Pasternak, Ceel. *Cool Careers for Girls in Construction.* Manassas Park, Va.: Impact Publications, 2000.

Peterson's. *Peterson's Summer Opportunities for Kids & Teenagers.* 24th ed. Lawrenceville, N.J.: Peterson's, 2006.

Salvadori, Mario. *The Art of Construction: Projects and Principles for Beginning Engineers and Architects.* 3rd ed. Chicago: Chicago Review Press, 2000.

Sterrett, Andrew (ed.). *101 Careers in Mathematics.* 2nd ed. Washington, D.C.: Mathematical Association of America, 2003.

Sumichrast, Michael. *Opportunities in Building Construction Careers.* New York: McGraw-Hill, 2007.

Thomas, Mark. *A Day with a Bricklayer.* New York: Children's Press, 2000.

Woods, Michael, and Mary B. Woods. *Ancient Construction: From Tents to Towers.* Minneapolis: Runestone Press, 2000.

Woods, Michael, and Mary B. Woods. *Ancient Machines: From Wedges to Waterwheels*. Minneapolis: Runestone Press, 1999.

Web Sites

A+ Math
http://www.aplusmath.com

Alliant Energy Kids
http://www.powerhousekids.com

American Council for Construction Education
http://www.acce-hq.org

ARCHcareers.org
http://www.archcareers.org

CoolMath.com
http://coolmath.com

Energy Kid's Page
http://www.eia.doe.gov/kids/energyfacts/sources/electricity.html

Everything About Construction Equipment
http://www.kenkenkikki.jp/special/e_index.html

Junior Engineering Technical Society
http://jets.org

National Building Museum
http://www.nbm.org

National Center for Construction Education and Research
http://www.nccer.org

National Organization of Women in Construction
http://www.nawic.org

This Old House
http://www.thisoldhouse.com/toh

U.S. Department of Labor: Employment & Training Administration
http://www.doleta.gov/OA/eta_default.cfm